VERTICAL VIEWS

SILKSCREEN MONOPRINT COLLAGE

LOU STOVALL

Workshop, Inc.
3145 Newark St. NW
Washington, DC 20008

www.loustovall.com

This catalog was published in coordination with *Vertical Views: Silkscreen Monoprint Collage*, an exhibition of work by Lou Stovall on view at the Katzen Center, American University Museum, April 3 - May 20, 2012.

the KATZEN
AMERICAN UNIVERSITY MUSEUM
COLLEGE *of* ARTS & SCIENCES

Cover: *Gail's Garden, Spring*, 2012. Silkscreen monoprint collage. 25 1/4 x 25 1/4 in.
Opposite: *Sweet Tea*, 2012. Silkscreen monoprint. 32 x 51 1/2 in.
Page 4: *Sally's Field, Planted*, 2012. Silkscreen monoprint. 32 x 51 1/2 in.
Page 6: *Lapis*, 2011. Silkscreen monoprint collage. 25 1/4 x 25 1/4 in. Collection of the Art Bank, DC Commission on the Arts and Humanities.
Page 8: *Southern Skies, West*, 2012. Silkscreen monoprint collage. 25 1/4 x 25 1/4 in.
Page 17: *Orchidaceous, Minor*, 2012. Silkscreen monoprint collage. 25 1/4 x 25 1/4 in.
Page 18: *Rock Creek Center*, 2011. Silkscreen monoprint collage. 25 1/4 x 25 1/4 in.
Page 23: *Roses X*, 2012. Silkscreen monoprint collage. 25 1/4 x 25 1/4 in.
Page 24: *Roses XII*, 2012. Silkscreen monoprint collage. 25 1/4 x 25 1/4 in.

Photography by John Woo and Greg Staley
Editing and book design by Anne C. Smith
Printed by CPS Gumpert, Annapolis and Hunt Valley, MD.

Text set in Lato by Łukasz Dziedzic.
Measurements indicate size of art framed.

ISBN: 978-0-615-62085-5

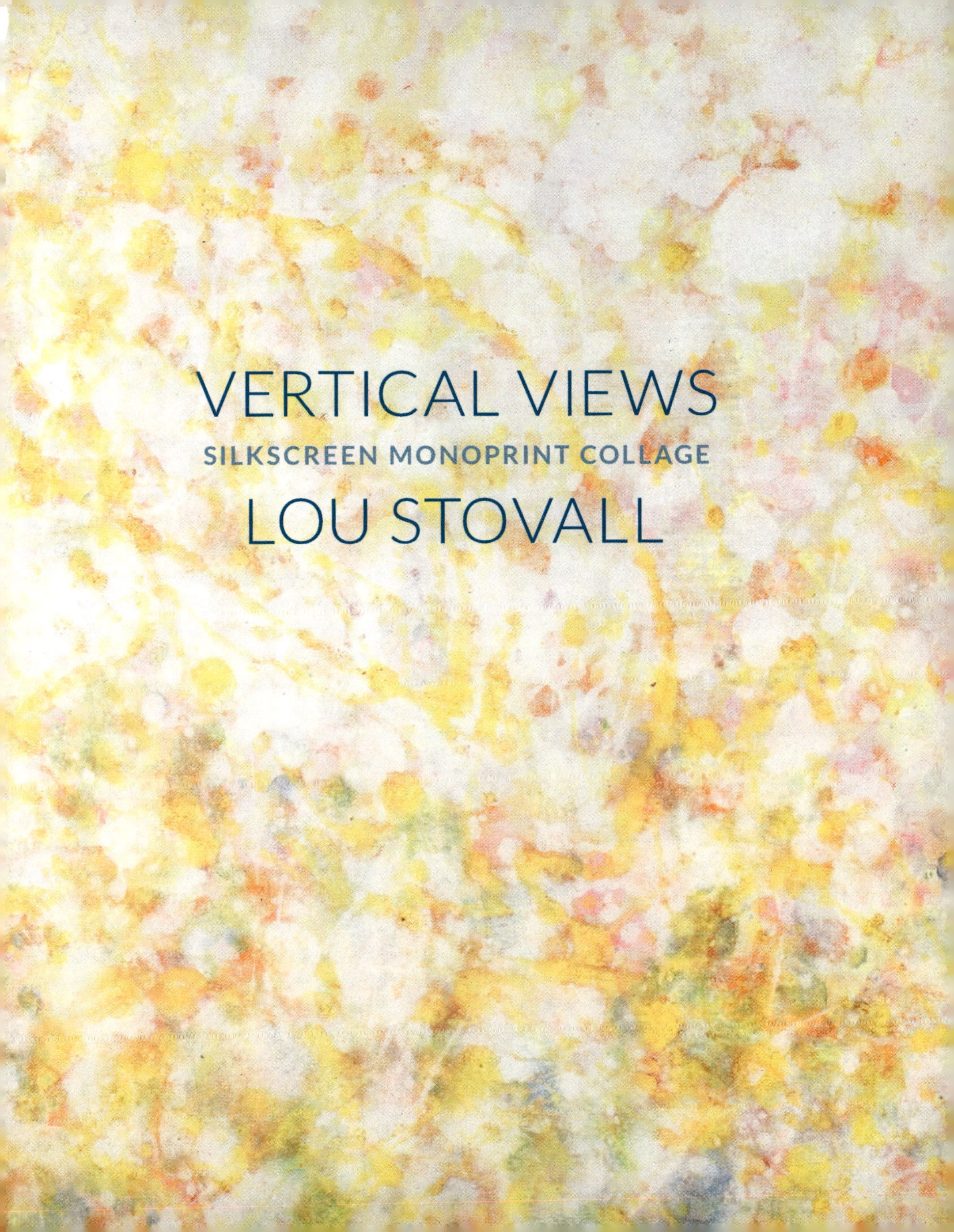

VERTICAL VIEWS

SILKSCREEN MONOPRINT COLLAGE

LOU STOVALL

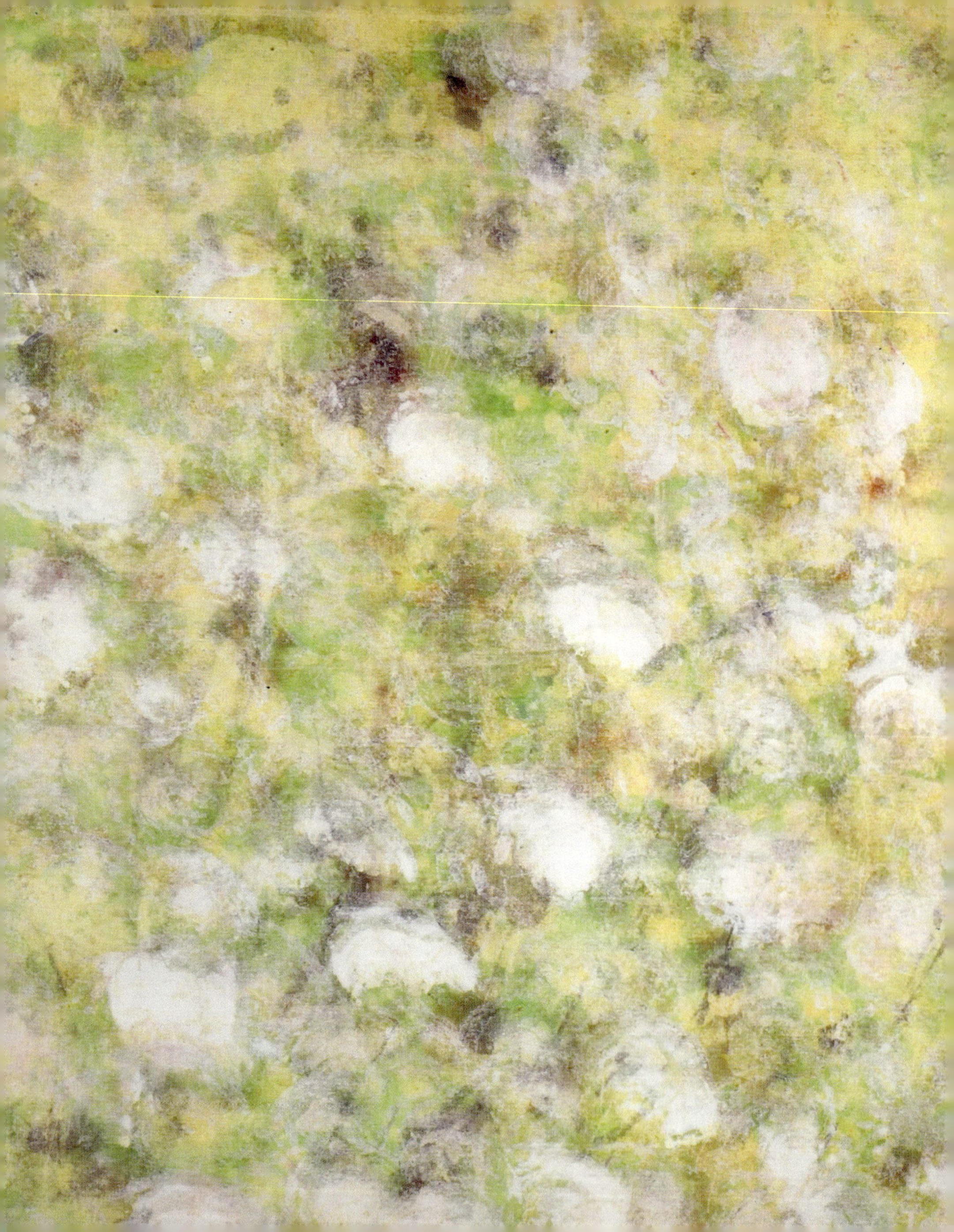

To our great, loving friend
and long-standing opera mentor,

SALLY BOASBERG

I dedicate this catalog and the monoprint,
Sally's Field, Planted

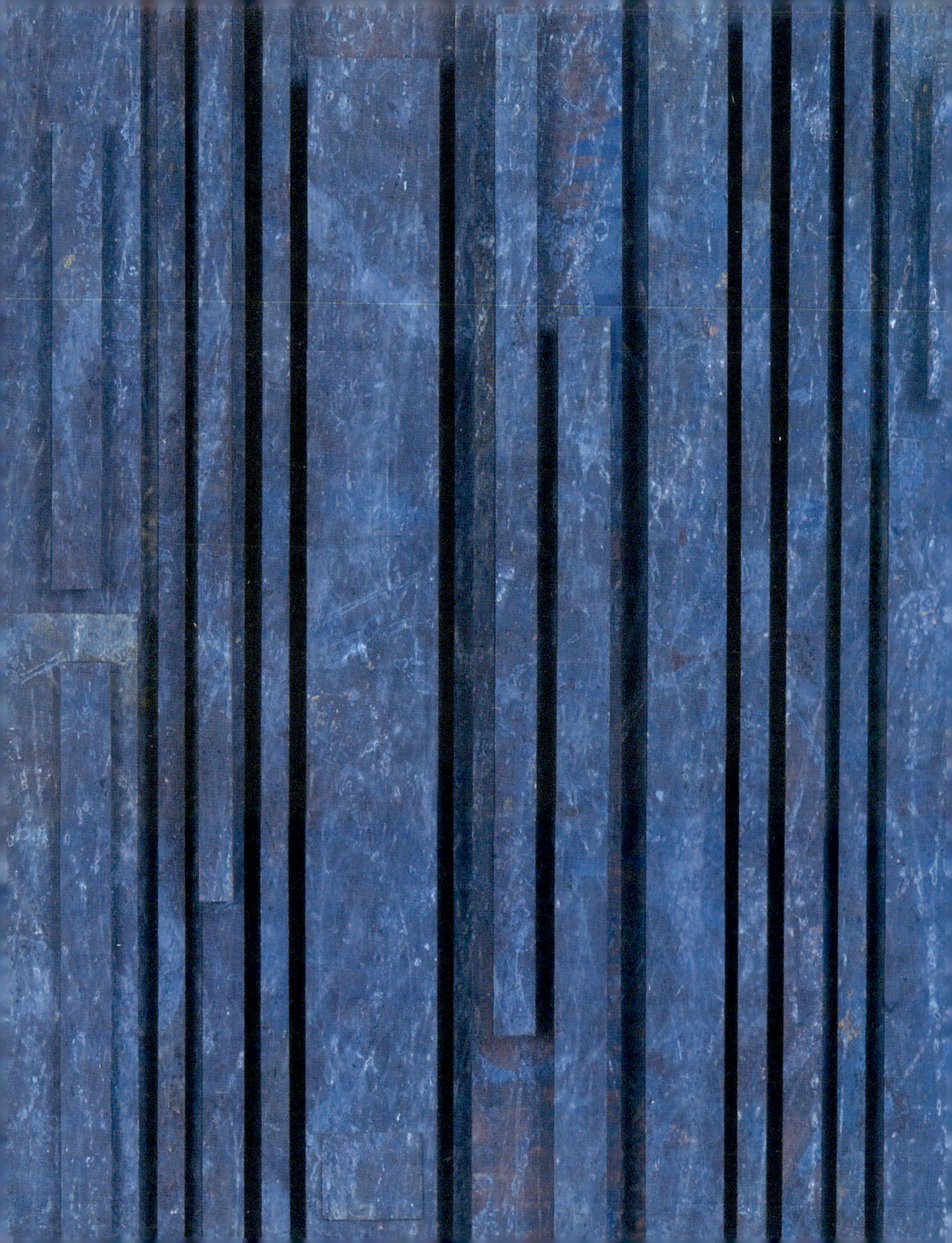

INTRODUCTION

PETER STARR

AMERICAN UNIVERSITY HAS a history of reaching out to prominent artists and educators in Washington, DC's, cultural community, who generously share their history and experiences in the arts, for the benefit of our students and friends alike.

Lou Stovall has been associated with American University for the past 35 years. He has contributed work to the AU Museum collection and served for many years on our AU Arts Council. A master printmaker, Lou has made collaborative prints with an outstanding array of local artists who also have a long history with AU, including Sam Gilliam, Gene Davis, Willem de Looper and Minnie Klavens. And Lou has been an invaluable partner and sounding board as we seek to involve our neighbors more closely in the vibrant life of the arts at AU.

As dean of AU's College of Arts and Sciences, I am deeply proud of our long association with such a warm and talented artist and friend of the university and take great pleasure in introducing Lou Stovall's *Vertical Views.*

Peter Starr
dean, College of Arts and Sciences
American University

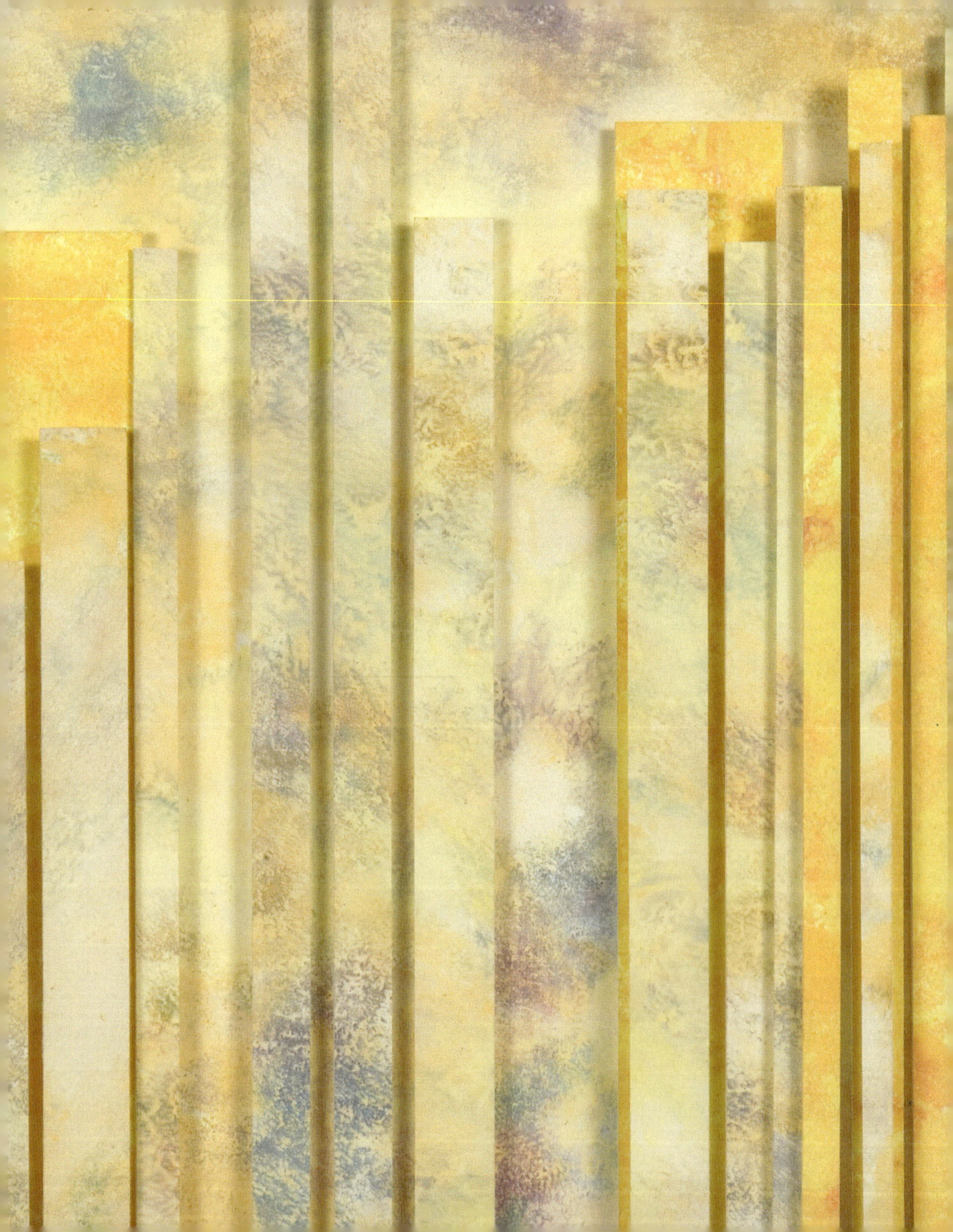

VERTICAL VIEWS: NOTES ON THE VIEWS

LOU STOVALL

FIRST THE LINE, gently drawn as in a beginning; a morning's sunrise, light coming just over a gentle rise of earth from its origin, New England, the source of my youth, a place where a life could begin. I have written these words before as parts of my being, certainly my beginning, and the origin of self. In my poem, *Morning and I are of a Mind,*[1] I wrote, "Green rich velvet earth rolling along...gently into a stand of old oaks and out again... where the sun is filling out the day with warming strokes." This is the stuff of my dreams. A moment of thought follows that first line. Later, hundreds and hundreds, often thousands of gestural marks and lines embrace the idea of a land where life can be lived at a pleasurable tempo; a land that exists perpetually in my thoughts. It is a vision I continually long to draw and a place where I would like to be. Therein lies my passion for drawing and making silkscreen prints.

A LINE IS A DOT THAT WENT FOR A WALK.

– PAUL KLEE

SWISS ARTIST (1879–1940)

As I stand before the open silkscreen, I find myself yielding to that inner expanse of landscape. It happens every time, but it is always new; just as the silkscreen is my constant medium, the experience of printing always takes me to a new place. This time, I begin my journey there by painting directly on the screen. Where I once cut dozens, sometimes hundreds, of stencils to create whole editions of identical prints, my monoprints are one-of-a-kind and made without the use of cut stencils. The gestures and colors of ink that I pour onto the screen and print on rag paper can never be recreated in exactly the same way; each impression is unique to the piece and each piece will go through many passes under the screen over a period of days, weeks, or months. Subsequent passes enhance the subtlety of the beginning image. The resulting image is, in one sense, a history or record of my movements over the screen. But the overall impact of the final image references other themes entirely—a quiet glade, a rush of wings overhead, and the formation of winsome clouds.

I have been enamored of the landscape throughout my career—the harmony and completeness of a landscape is owed to the coexistence of many parts which are beautiful and engaging, very much like a musical experience. While nature's beautiful forms are often fleeting, art will last. My prints and drawings are meant to celebrate the life and energy which a single blossom can hold, to communicate my vision, work, and optimism as the elixir of my life.

My inclinations to stand and see, to look and wonder, and to write and draw are counterpoints to one another and sustain one another as such. I believe if one is to understand the wonder of a waterfall, it is helpful to stand still to watch the water, to hear the sounds, and to feel the mist from the falling water. Such observations hold expectancy of thoughtful action. At times the act of making art fuels an idea and energizes a theme, but most often, the action of making art sustains my desire to write prose about the process. Once my motivation is in motion, my thoughts are not confined to the single work before me. Instead, the desire to sing, dance, and compose verse adds to the fullness of the creative experience. Perhaps that is the reason so many artists prefer to work alone. At the height of creativity, the artist is both performer and audience. The act of making art is like a stage production. For the seasoned artist, writing may also be a self generating experience. As an artist, the essential application of Descartes' philosophy, "I think, therefore

I am," is to make my whole self available to all the possibilities of personal creativity. In fact, my need to be an artist is as persistent as the desire to express myself in words.

Images and messages infuse my thoughts while creating. My imagination leads me to embellish the simple form to make a gentle gesture. A gracious flow of energy takes my lines and spaces to places of warmth and romance. The afterthought of a comely line brings a smile as I hold my breath to savor the moment. My monoprints speak to me in terms of wholeness; they have a resonance that makes them complete as they are and represent the essential vision that I had in mind when I began. These are usually the images which suggest places where I might like to be. They take my thoughts to places once visited or imagined—a field of roses on a sun-drenched Southern California hill or an abstracted serendipitous version of Rock Creek Park, our in-city forest.

But I could not resist my spirit of adventure. I began to think how to go deeper into space as I have in my pencil drawings. The use of perspective has always been a fascination, so I began to develop the idea of collage. Experimenting with some prints by cutting them into strips and reassembling the pieces allowed me to construct interior images, reminiscent of entering a wooded glade with leaves swaying in a gentle breeze and sunlight streaming between the trunks.

Beginning with a large abstract rectangular print which may suggest a landscape or a field of color, I cut the monoprint into strips which will be reassembled into a vertical view; these strips will become the building blocks for the collage. They are mounted on pieces of bass wood, which I cut to fit the printed strips. The real discovery and wonder happens in recombining the strips, finding just the right order and just the right height such that these various individual elements act in concert with one another and become a whole, unified piece again. Striving to maintain the vertical look and feel of each piece is an important challenge. I relish the beautiful relationship between colors and the de-stabilization of the static or geometric form; in other words, the interplay or flux of areas becomes a counterpoint to verticality similar to a musical "call and response."

As I compose these three-dimensional, vertical collages, the action that takes place during the cutting, choosing, and assembling of the cut-up monoprint is not unlike the stage production I described. I am, in a sense, performing the creation of a new image at the same time that I am witnessing, as the enthralled audience, a new terrain unfolding before me.

Inevitably, the creation of each piece holds a surprise and a new discovery for me. Dashes of red or splatters of blue that acted one way in the original print take on new relationships and new roles when they are recombined as a collage. Certain colors or elements may find that they must play a supporting role while others are brought forward into prominence. What were once separate, disparate, or random patterns begin to associate to create abstract but recognizable images of *vertical views*. Dissolving or reinforcing the geometry and verticality of the collage's construction, they seek to belong together as in a musical movement or poetic prose.

Often enough, the specific titles come after the composition. Discussions and observations with my wife Di Stovall bring titles from travel, poetry, and memories. These titles take on the spirit of certain prints, such as *Sweet Tea* and *Apricot Afternoon*. The title *Orchidaceous*—meaning showy and ostentatious—is pure fun. Gerard Manley Hopkins, my favorite poet, wrote, "Glory be to God for dappled things"[2]—hence *Dappled Things*. *Gail's Garden* comes from a walk with our friend Gail to her favorite patch of landscape where leaves sway in the gentle breeze. And, of course, my friend Sally Boasberg, who has planted and nurtured so much more beyond the incredible array of flowers and trees that fill her garden and ours, inspired the print, *Sally's Field, Planted*. The pursuit of the landscape is therefore a journey just as patches of fields are places of rest and contemplation. My ever-present preoccupation is to suggest the landscape through fields of color. Color and memory guide my creation of rhythm and movement that ultimately causes feelings of harmonious creativity and shared beauty.

Lou Stovall
master printmaker

[1] Lou Stovall, *Morning and I are of a Mind*, written 1974, published in *Lou Stovall: Artist and the Landscape* by City of Charleston Office of Cultural Affairs, in conjunction with International Arts & Artists, 2008.

[2] Gerard Manley Hopkins, *Pied Beauty*, 1918.

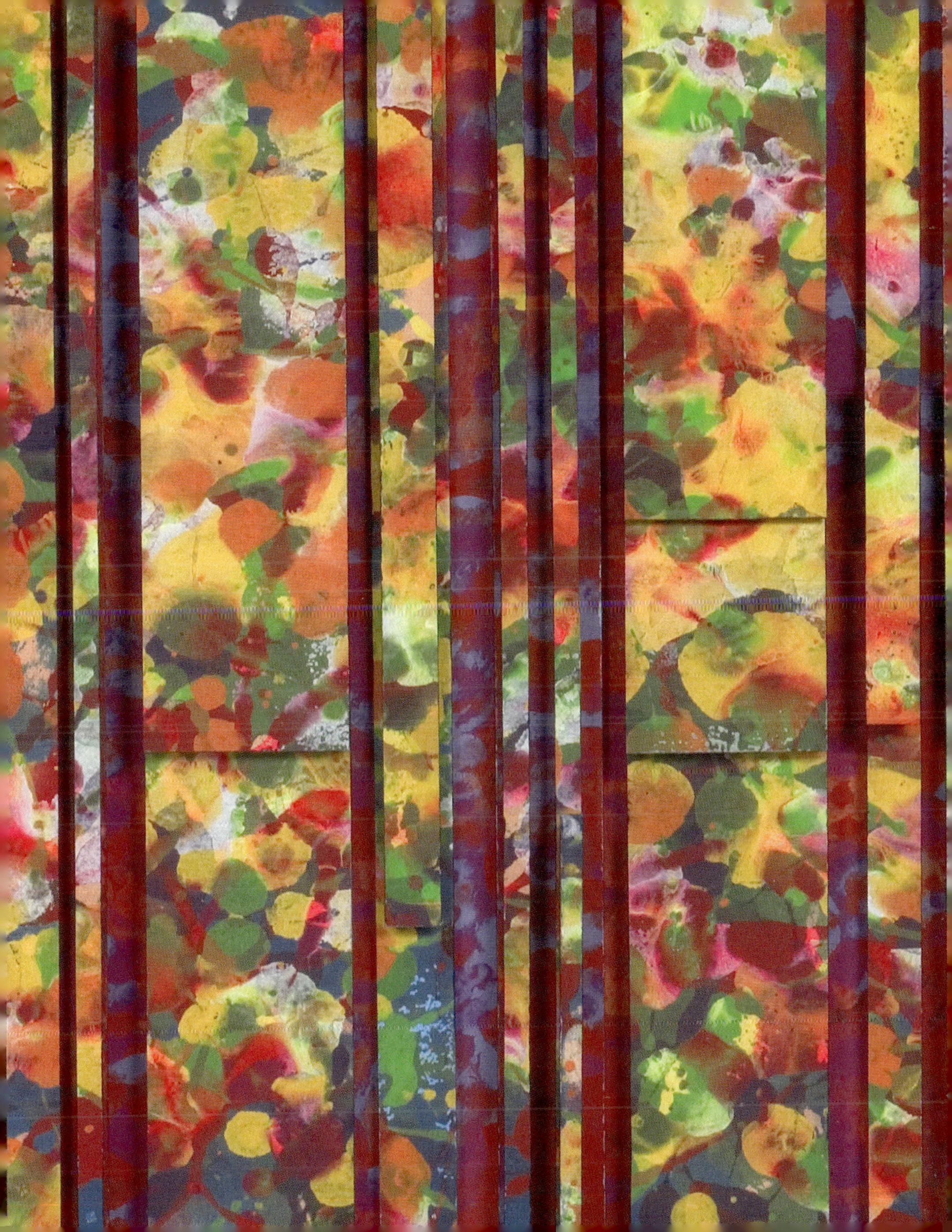

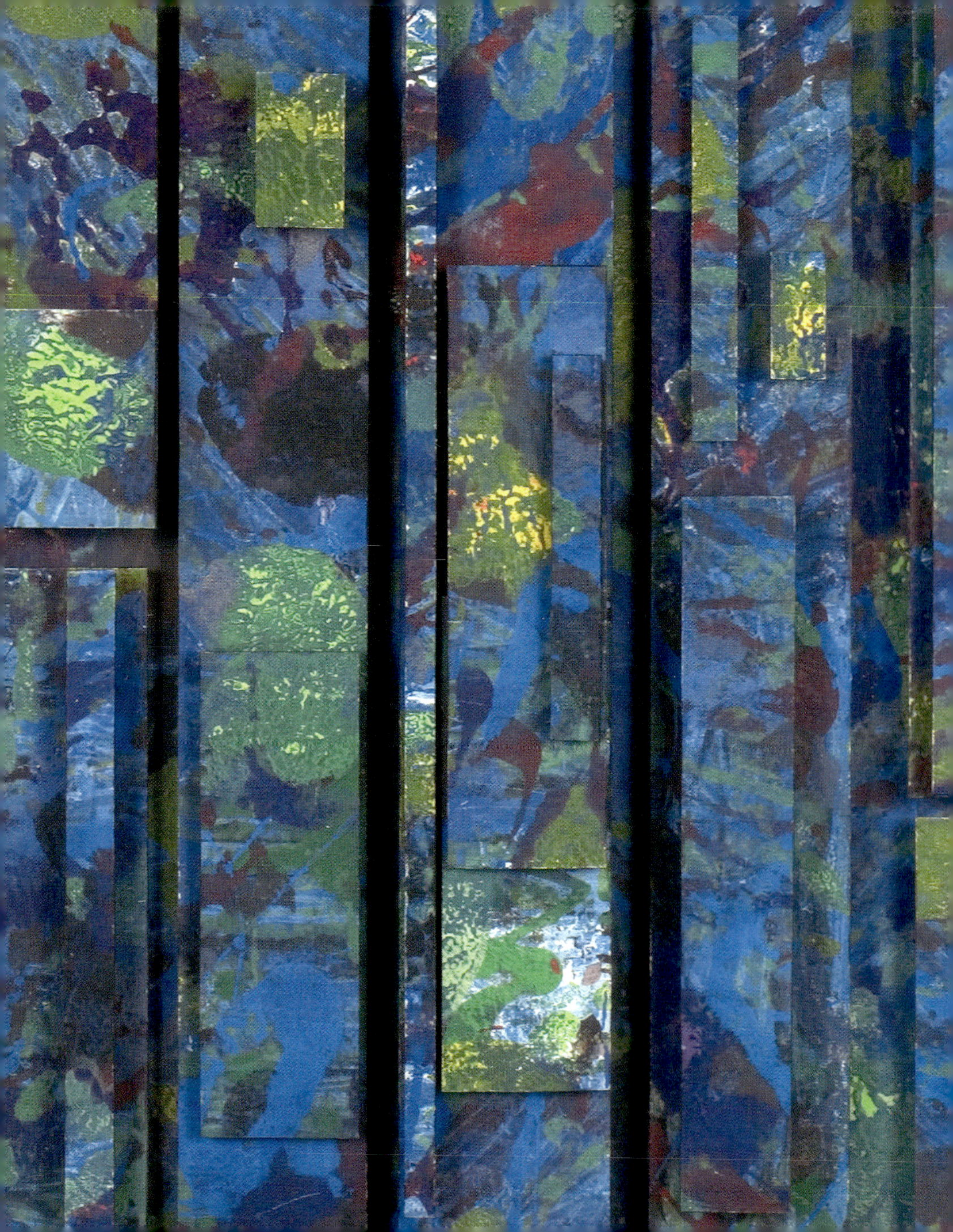

WORKING WITH LOU STOVALL: A LESSON IN CHANCE

ANNE C. SMITH

TO SEE LOU print on the silkscreen is to see an artist in focused conversation with his own work. As his assistant, I have had the opportunity to observe Lou at work on his monoprints, and I have come to see his process as one of give-and-take. First, Lou moves. He applies ink directly to the screen in fine sprays of yellow or broad drops of green. Then, the ink. It seems to respond to his actions in its own wonderfully unexpected way, as it drifts and pools and suggests the next step in a series of layered color and texture. And so, Lou responds. The print responds. A veritable tango of creation follows—action and reaction—until the print achieves that mysterious, serendipitous state called finished.

Lou's approach to his work is a reminder that discovery happens when one tries new things, looks for the unexpected, and takes risks. Since he began printing at the age of fifteen, Lou has acquired an intricate knowledge about the behavior of color and materials and still maintains a fresh curiosity for untested, uncharted methods to make his best work possible. He is on one hand operating with a massive wealth of experience and knowledge while also remaining open to accident and chance. This is the best attitude an artist can have.

The *Vertical Views* in this exhibition are a case in point. We can all imagine that to cut up one's own work takes a certain amount of trust in oneself and the acceptance of failure if all does not turn out as planned. But the risk Lou took when he first cut up one of his two-dimensional monoprints to rebuild as a three-dimensional collage allowed him to evolve his understanding of landscape, rhythm, and color, not to mention the fundamental question of what, exactly, a silkscreen print can do and be. Lou's early landscapes are dramatically different from his current work—in format, technique, and style. And yet these vertical views can be traced directly to his early work through a series of fruitful risks and innovations.

Now, while Lou may take risks, he is by no means reckless. Anyone who has interacted with Lou, or who knows him very well, will laugh at the idea of a haphazard Lou Stovall (even the man behind the fish counter who, while selling Lou a piece of salmon, held up a fillet for his approval, only to watch as Lou pulled out his tape measure to make sure the fillet was the size he wanted. To Lou, a measurement in inches—down to the thirty-second of an inch—reigns king.)

Some months ago, I came into the studio to see that Lou had finished a monoprint which was bathed in the softest shades of white and yellow and green and orange—all so light and effervescent that the effect of the print was ethereal and warm, like looking at the sun diffused through a freshly laundered sheet. Was the print finished? It could have been. The print held together by such a delicate balance of color and light that to put it back under the screen was a considerable risk. But it was a risk that Lou took. The print today, titled *Sweet Tea*, retains that light, sunny feeling, but has taken on an additional intensity that makes it what I regard as one of Lou's most complex monoprints. I made a mental note of his leap of faith.

What Lou's work shows, over the years, is that he has remained open to new ideas and motivated in the pursuit of new techniques and interpretations of his recurring subjects. The collages on view come from a wellspring all their own, drawing from six decades of handling silkscreen ink, pulling the squeegee, looking, and trusting instincts. Lou's ability to work in a spirit of openness and awareness is a model for me. As Lisa Farrell, a former assistant of Lou's and current graphic designer in the Department of Design and Installation at the National Gallery of Art, said, "After working with Lou, I could have been a carpenter, a printmaker, a conservation picture framer, any number of things.... Most importantly, he taught what is meant by the artist's spirit. That's probably the strongest thing about Lou, his feeling and compassion for art."[3] What Lou teaches is *how* to be a creative person in any field; how to be one who discovers.

Anne C. Smith
studio assistant to Lou Stovall

[3] Lisa Farrell, telephone conversation with Ruth Fine, Curator of Modern Prints and Drawings, National Gallery of Art, 22 May 2002.

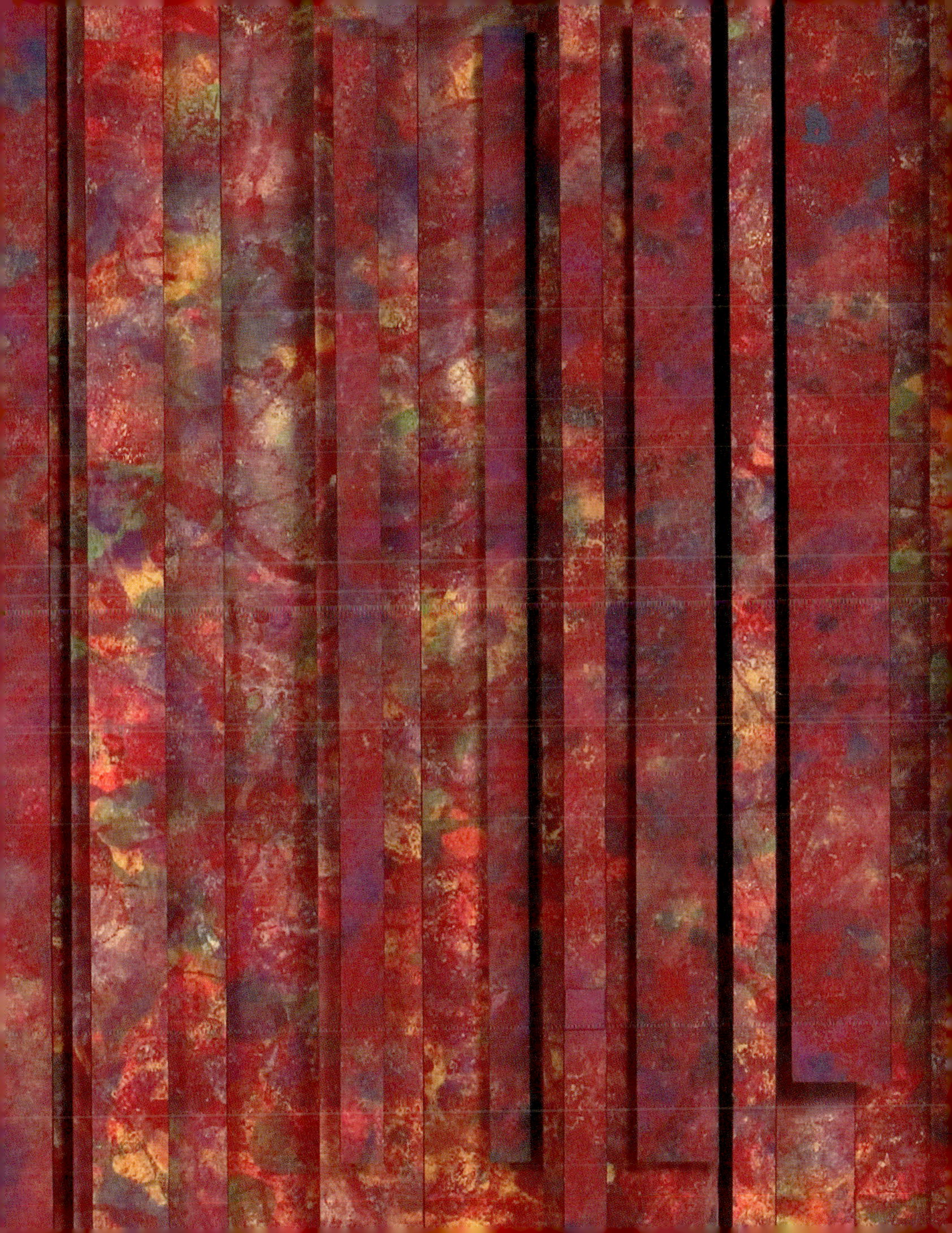

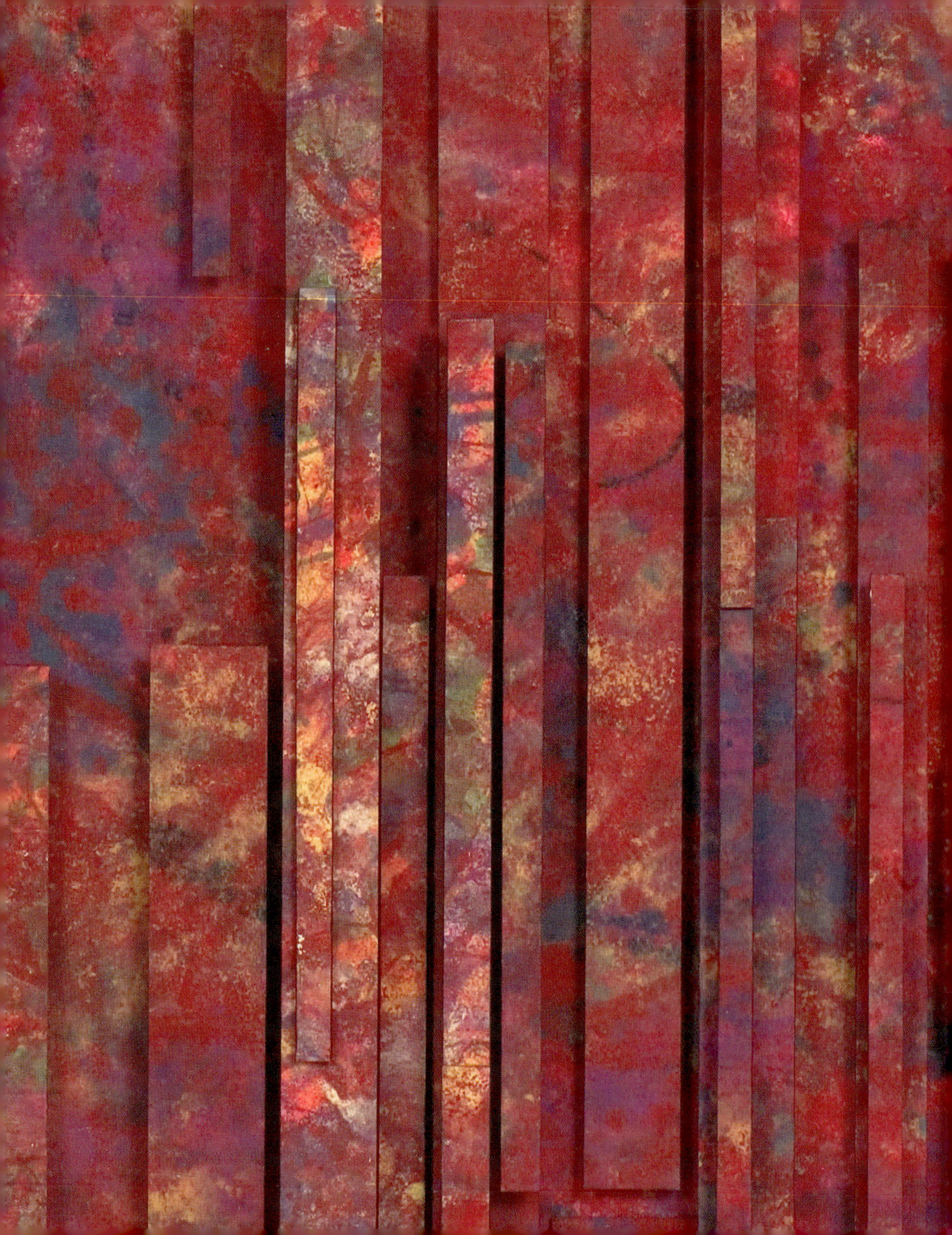

ALCHEMY

CHRISTOPHER ADDISON

LOU STOVALL PRINTS the way many artists paint. Except that his prints have the quality of veils of light. Since the 1960s, Lou has painted his prints through more and more refined filters, drawing on the spirit of his collaborations with artists like Elizabeth Catlett, Gene Davis, Sam Gilliam, Jacob Lawrence, Lois Mailou Jones, and Paul Reed, his proximity to and deep involvement with the Washington Color School and a complete mastery of the nature of silkscreen color applications and overlays.

Often, visits to the Workshop find Lou surrounded by music, the music of Leonard Cohen more recently, opera generally and, for a long period, Richard Einhorn's *Voices of Light*. That accompaniment, the soundtrack to the whirl of activity that is often found in the studio, characterizes the depth of feeling this artist is capable of delivering through his art. That music, like the conversation that is never lacking here, is an invitation to view the world through the artist's eyes. Visits with Lou bring words by Rainer Maria Rilke to mind, "For the sake of a few lines one must see many cities, men and things. One must know the animals, one must feel how the birds fly and know the gesture with which the small flowers open in the morning.... For it is not yet the memories themselves. Not until they have turned to blood within us, to glance, to gesture, nameless and no longer to be distinguished from ourselves—not until then can it happen that in a most rare hour the first word of a verse arises in their midst and goes forth from them."[4] A poet himself, Lou crafts art works which most certainly evoke images in the open ended manner of poetry and, without a doubt, memory has coalesced in him and gone forth in the forms of his art.

It has been a great pleasure to watch Lou Stovall's art change and evolve over the many years I have known him. This most recent body of work takes off on an exploration from a previous exhibition of idealized landscapes and vertical architecture. Each takes the viewer on a gentle stroll through an imagined place: a garden, a woods, a morning field, a rolling riverside. Each maintains a rigorous structure through which the eye can travel with grace and pleasure,

I THINK OF PAINTING WITHOUT SUBJECT MATTER AS MUSIC WITHOUT WORDS.

– KEN NOLAND

AMERICAN ARTIST (1924–2010)

parting veils, passing through to the enduring landscape of the artist's imagining. However, this fascination with landscape and deep love of the land is hardly new, has, in fact, been a constant to which the artist is here returning. One senses his deep delight in the endless permutations of place, his openness to wonder, and his reverence for the earth as a font of personal creativity.

"THE CREATIVE PROCESS LIES NOT IN IMITATING, BUT IN PARALLELING NATURE—TRANSLATING THE IMPULSE RECEIVED FROM NATURE INTO THE MEDIUM OF EXPRESSION, THUS VITALIZING THIS MEDIUM. THE PICTURE SHOULD BE ALIVE, THE STATUE SHOULD BE ALIVE, AND EVERY WORK OF ART SHOULD BE ALIVE."

- HANS HOFFMAN

GERMAN-AMERICAN ARTIST (1880–1966)

Strength, consistency, an exceptional color sense, developed over years of observation and experimentation, depth, precision, dedication to his craft, and an unerring sense of balance have been constants in Lou's work. In these *Views* the artist has taken another step in the alchemy of his art, transforming mundane materials into visual expressions. Reconstructing his own work, creating what he has referred to as a "call and response" attitude towards colors and the collaged forms, a fitting reference to early African-American blues and gospel music. Achieving, at the same time, on a field as dynamic as any Jackson Pollock work, a composition neatly hovering between control and chaos. This is magic indeed.

Also striking about these works is their modest scale. Like the artist, they are soft-spoken, with a depth and complexity which quietly commands attention. The works invite the viewer to wander through these vistas, to engage on an intimate scale and to imagine on their own. They suggest a microcosm of endless, percolating nature and an artist whose recycled, reinvented work is the ultimate creative compost. Yet despite modest scale their colors are vibrant, richly layered, and complex. They balance perfectly between a Pollock-like free expression and the ordered composition of Hans Hoffman, and they satisfy in the way a beloved landscape as it is touched by the new morning sun, made familiar with time, can. The best take root in your soul.

Christopher Addison
director, Addison/Ripley Gallery

[4] Rainer Maria Rilke, *The Notebooks of Malte Laurids Brigge*, 1910.

IMAGES

Calico, 2012
32 Silkscreen monoprint collage
25 1/4 x 25 1/4 in.

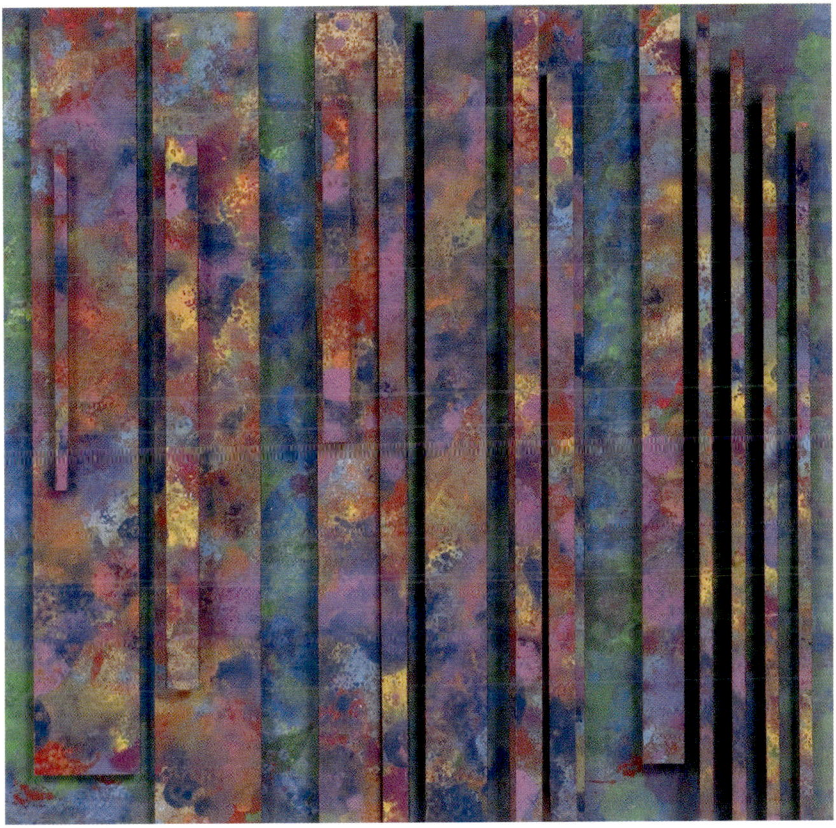

Operetta, 2011

34 Silkscreen monoprint collage

25 1/4 x 25 1/4 in.

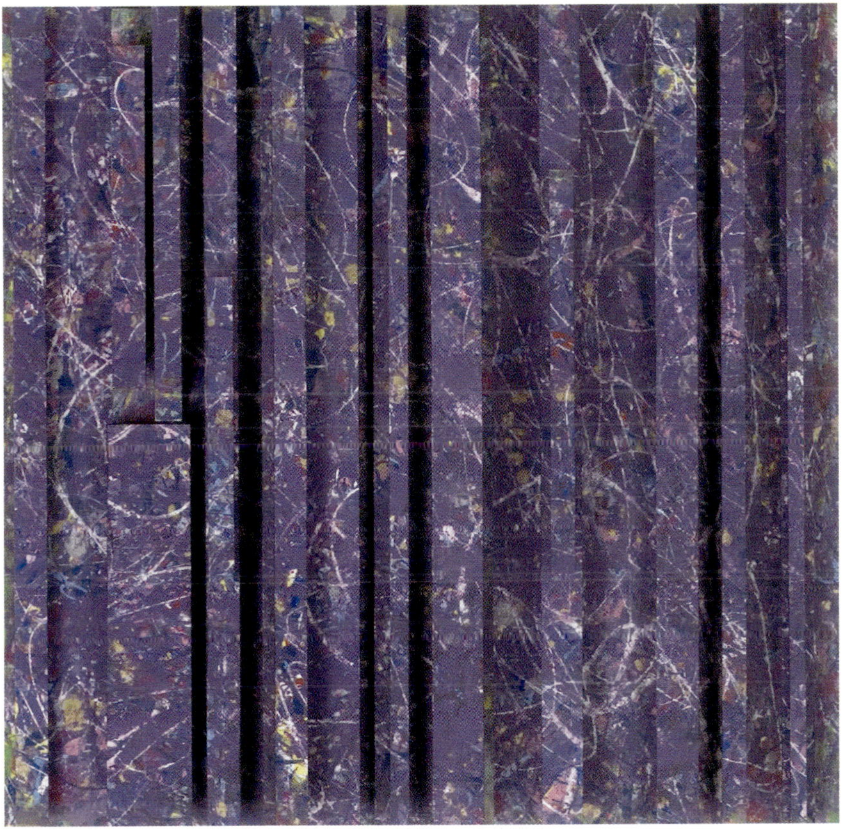

36

Azure, 2011
Silkscreen monoprint collage
25 1/4 x 25 1/4 in.
Collection of the Art Bank, DC Commission on the Arts and Humanities

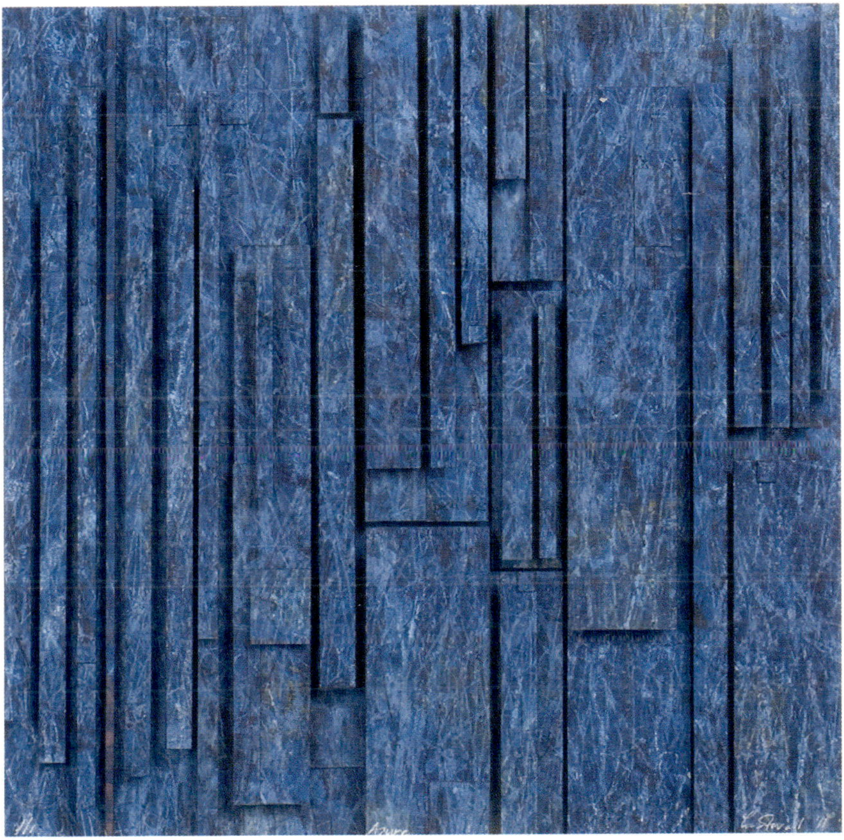
1/1
Azure

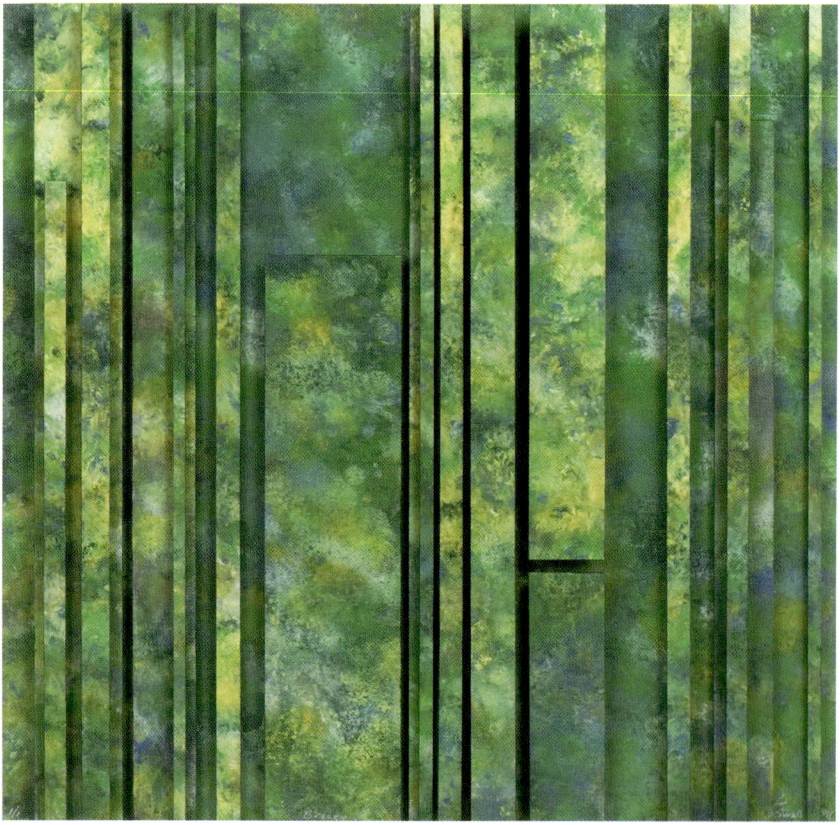

Breezy I, 2011
Silkscreen monoprint collage
25 1/4 x 25 1/4 in.
Collection of the Art Bank, DC Commission on the Arts and Humanities

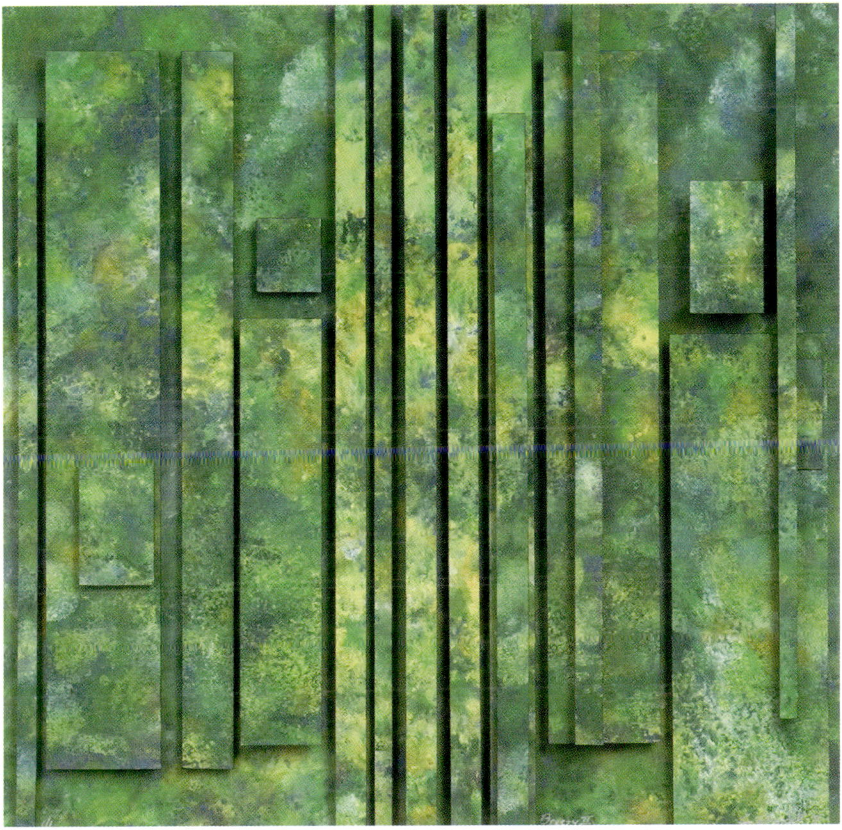

Breezy II, 2011
Silkscreen monoprint collage
25 1/4 x 25 1/4 in
Collection of the Art Bank, DC Commission on the Arts and Humanities.

Roses VI, 2011

40 Silkscreen monoprint collage

27 1/4 x 27 1/4 in.

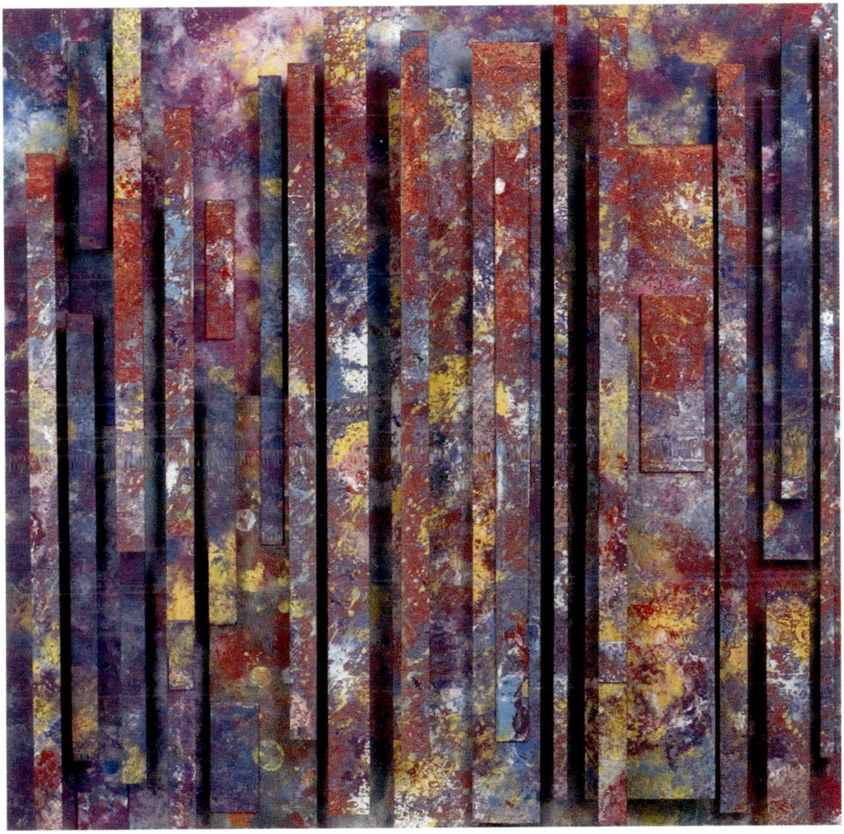

Roses IX, 2011
42 Silkscreen monoprint collage
26 1/4 x 26 1/4 in

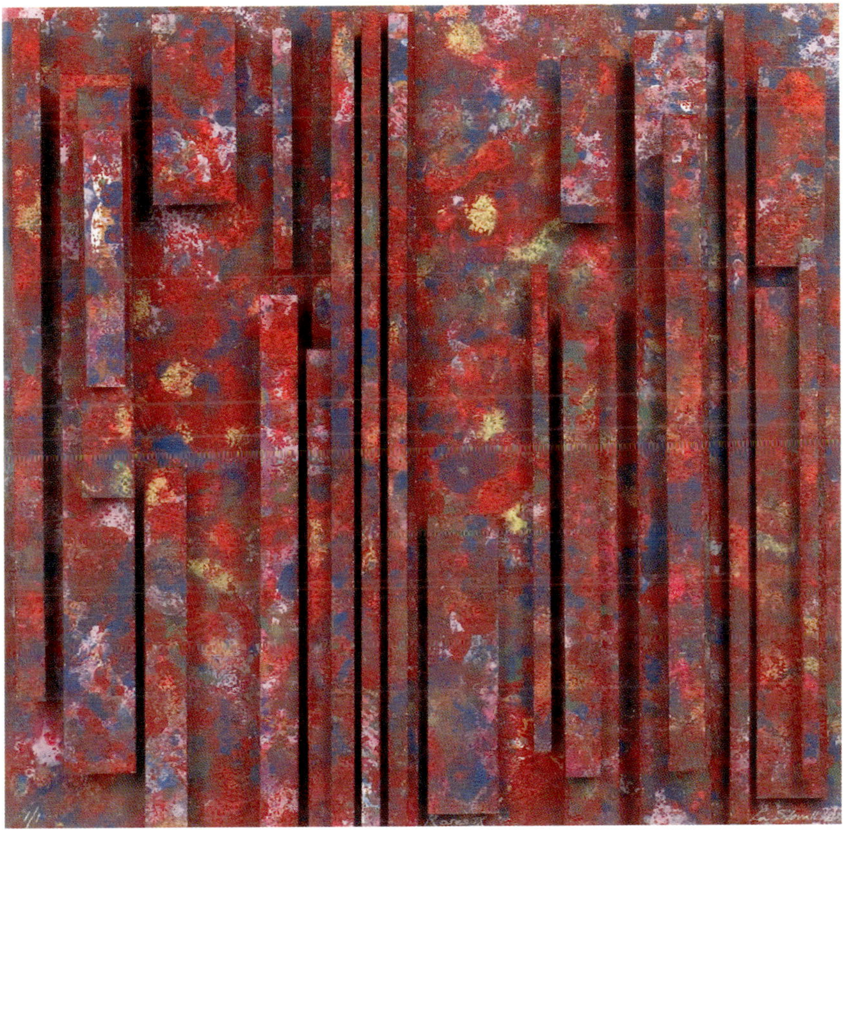

Roses X, 2012
44 Silkscreen monoprint collage
25 1/4 x 25 1/4 in.

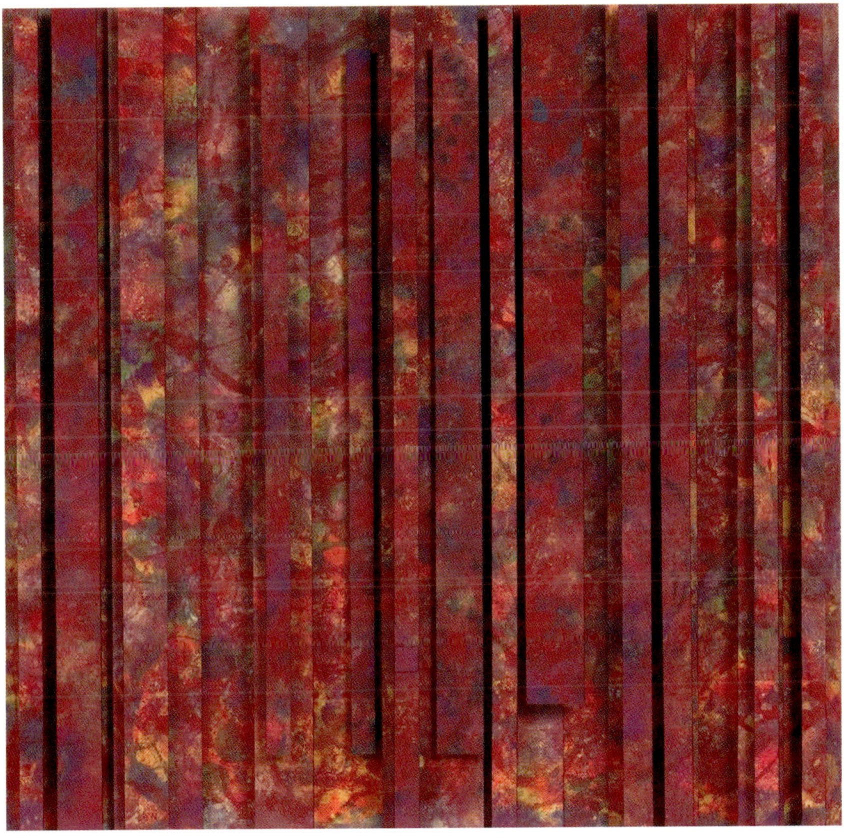

Rock Creek Center, 2011
46 Silkscreen monoprint collage
25 1/4 x 25 1/4 in.

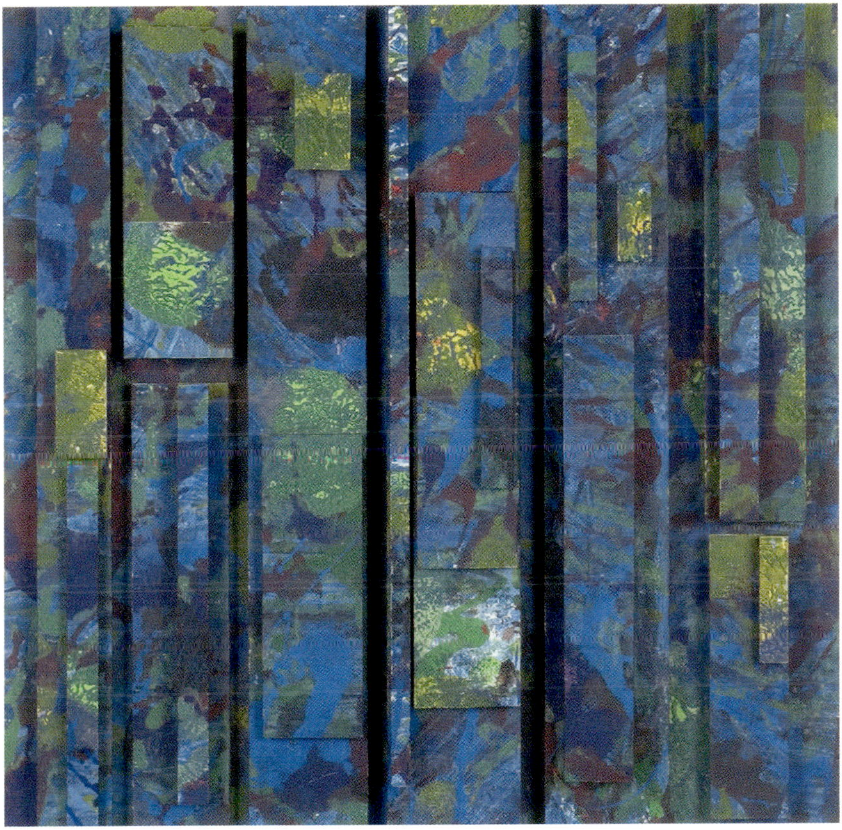

Lapis, 2011
Silkscreen monoprint collage
25 1/4 x 25 1/4 in.
Collection of the Art Bank, DC Commission on the Arts and Humanities

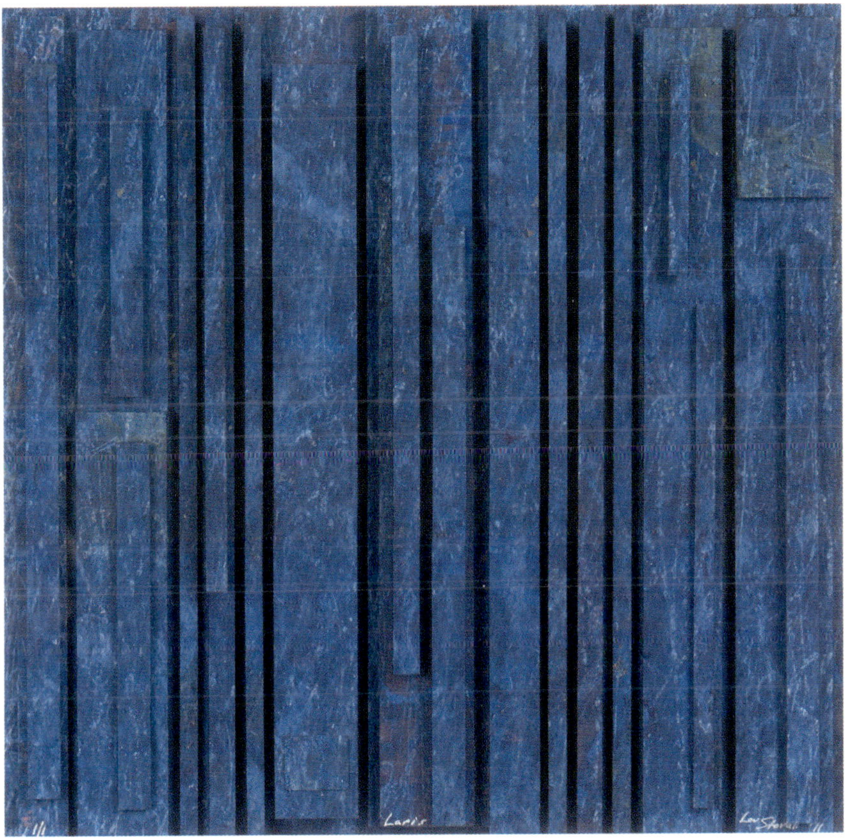
1/1
Lapis

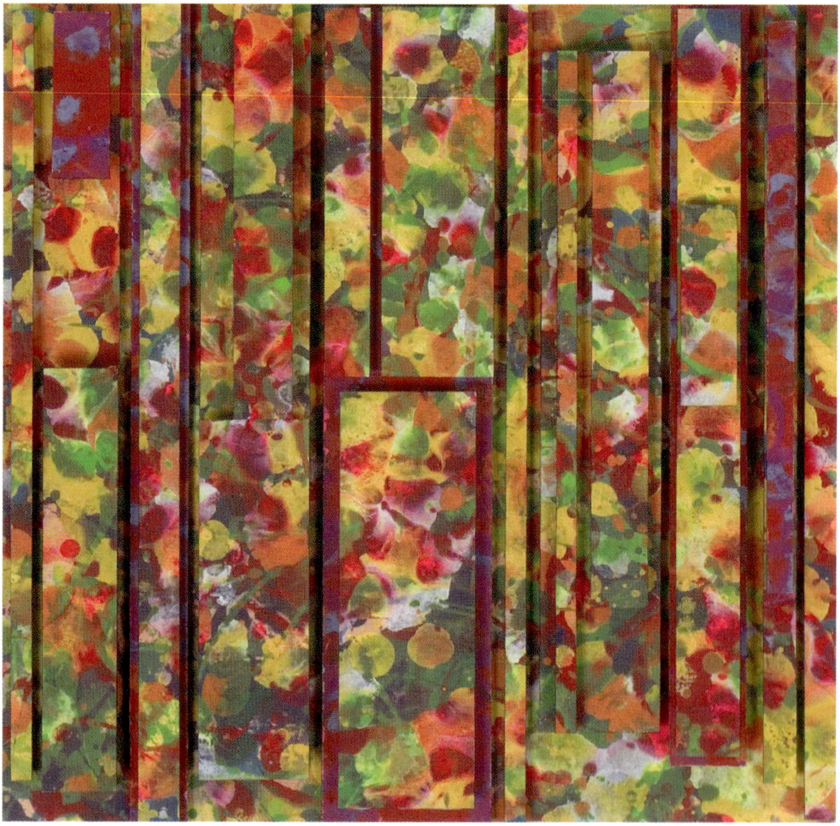

Orchidaceous, Major, 2012
Silkscreen monoprint collage
25 1/4 x 25 1/4 in.

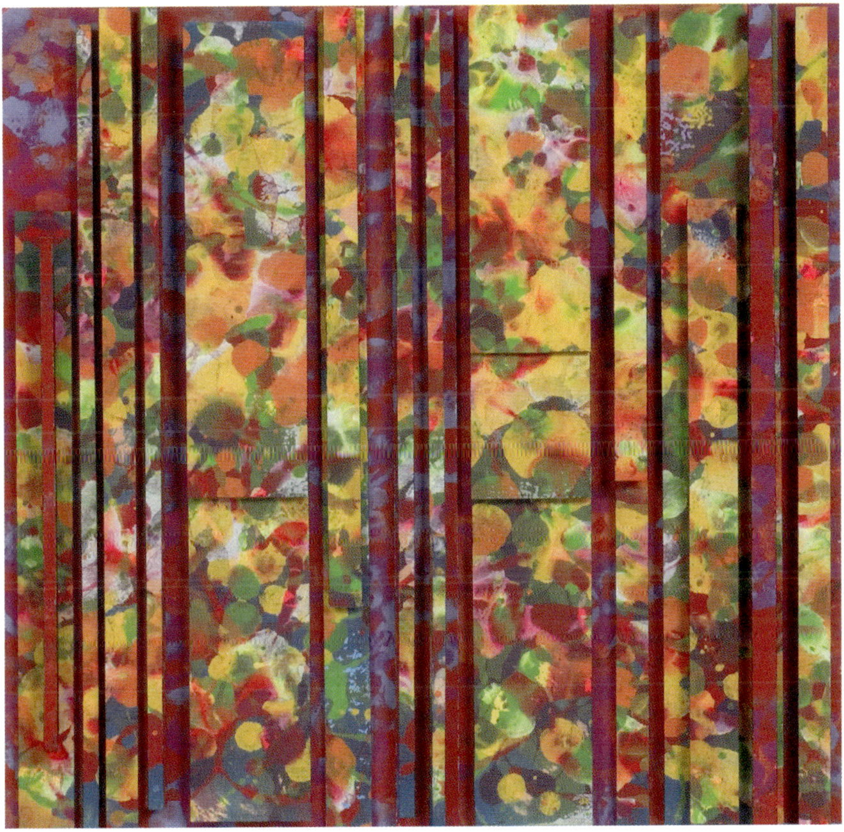

Orchidaceous, Minor, 2012
Silkscreen monoprint collage
25 1/4 x 25 1/4 in.

Roses XI, 2012

Silkscreen monoprint collage

25 1/4 x 25 1/4 in.

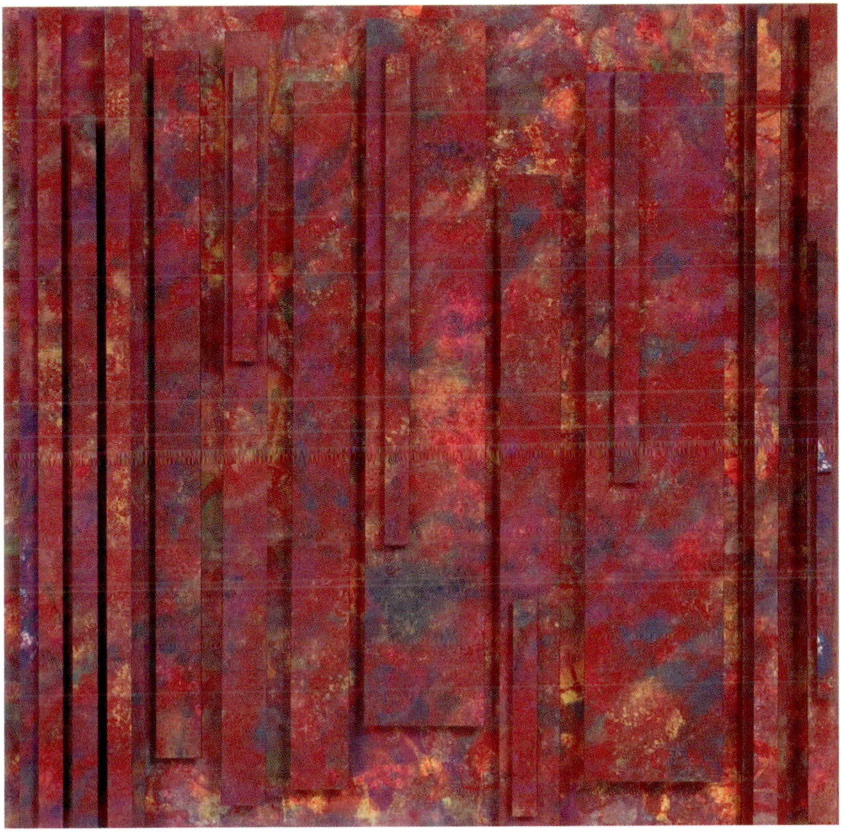

54

Roses XII, 2012
Silkscreen monoprint collage
25 1/4 x 25 1/4 in.

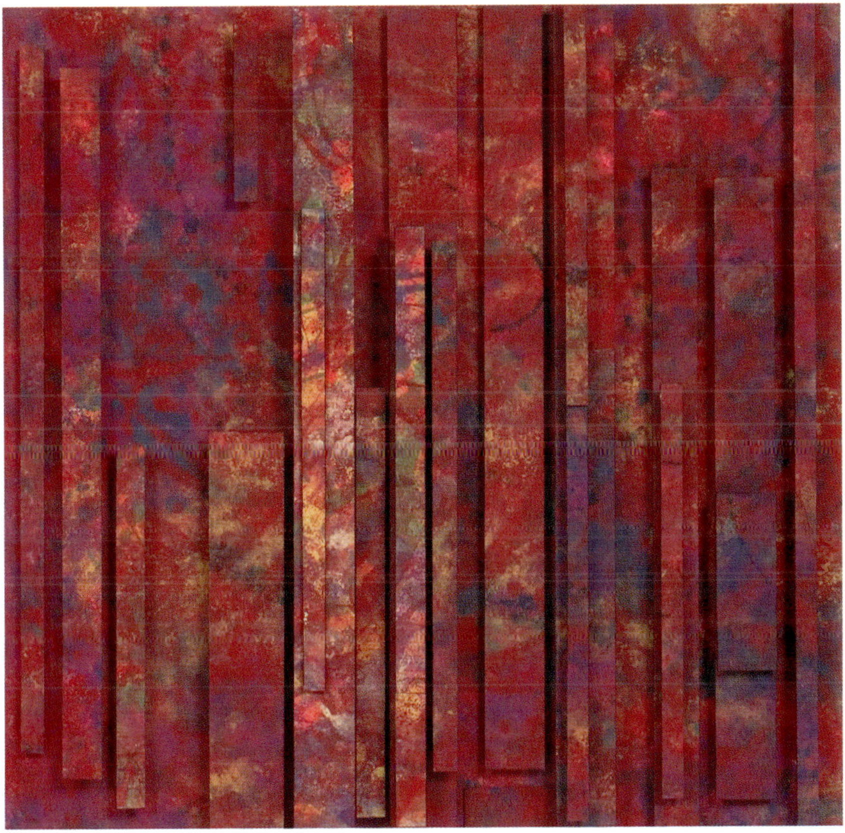

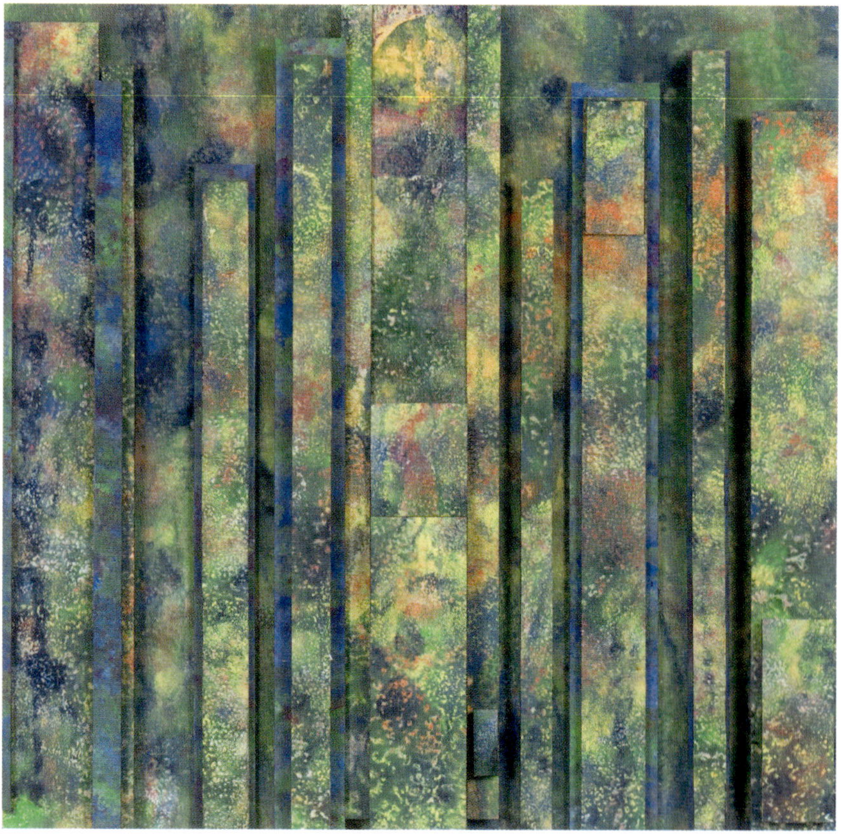

Gail's Garden, Spring, 2012

Silkscreen monoprint collage
25 1/4 x 25 1/4 in.

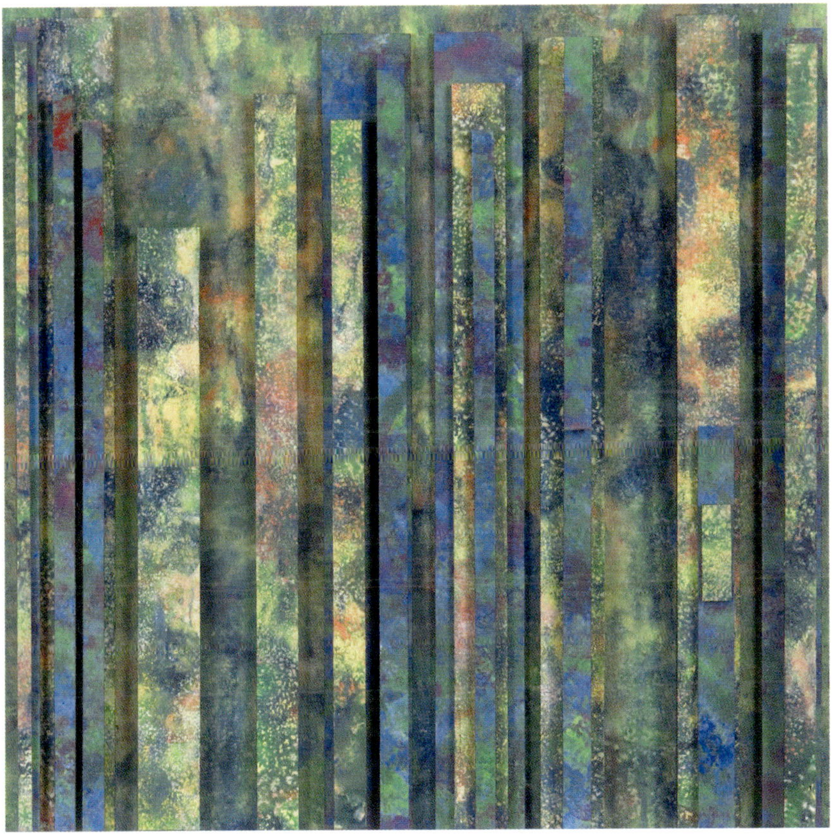

Gail's Garden, Summer, 2012
Silkscreen monoprint collage
25 1/4 x 25 1/4 in.

Southern Skies, East, 2012
58 Silkscreen monoprint collage
25 1/4 x 25 1/4 in.

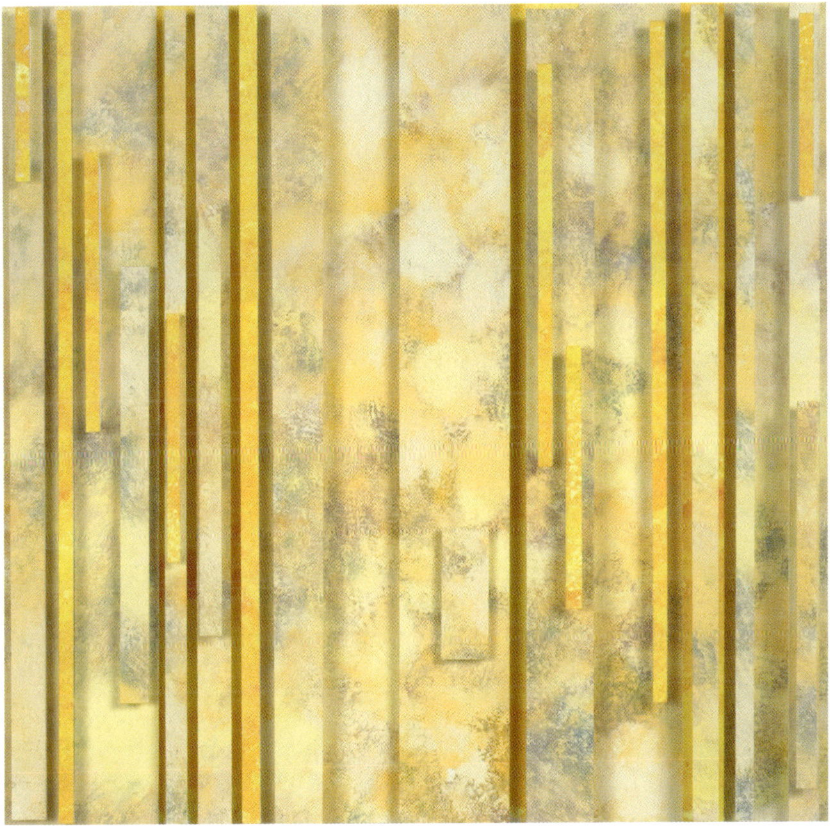

Southern Skies, West, 2012
Silkscreen monoprint collage
25 1/4 x 25 1/4 in.

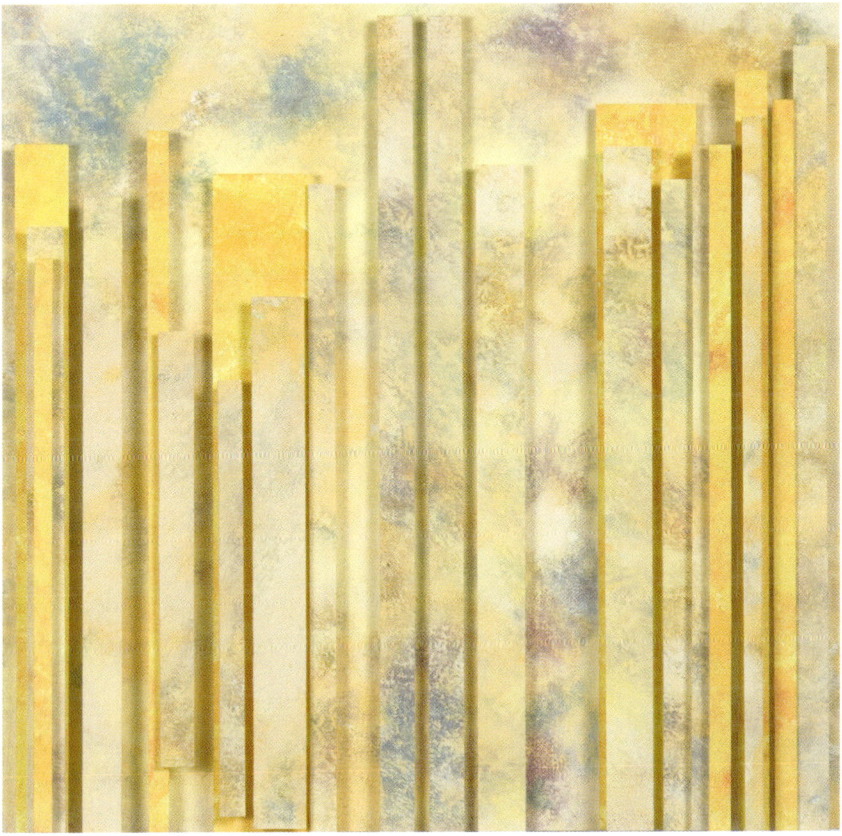

Dappled Things, 2012
Silkscreen monoprint collage
25 1/4 x 25 1/4 in.

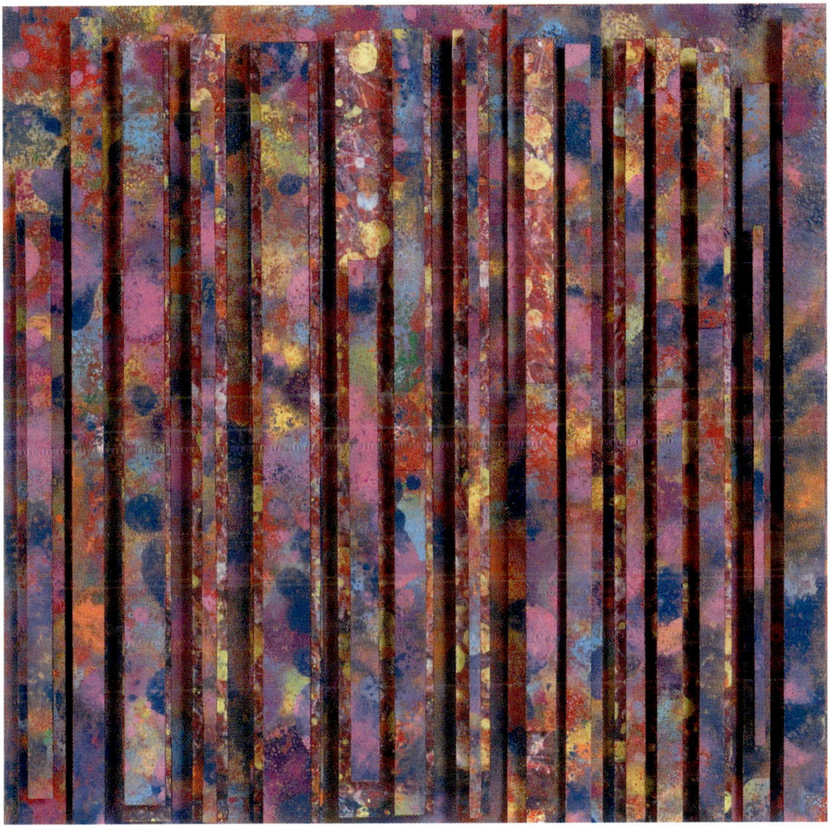

Song for Eva, 2009
Silkscreen monoprint collage
26 x 26 in.
Collection of Kate Pincus

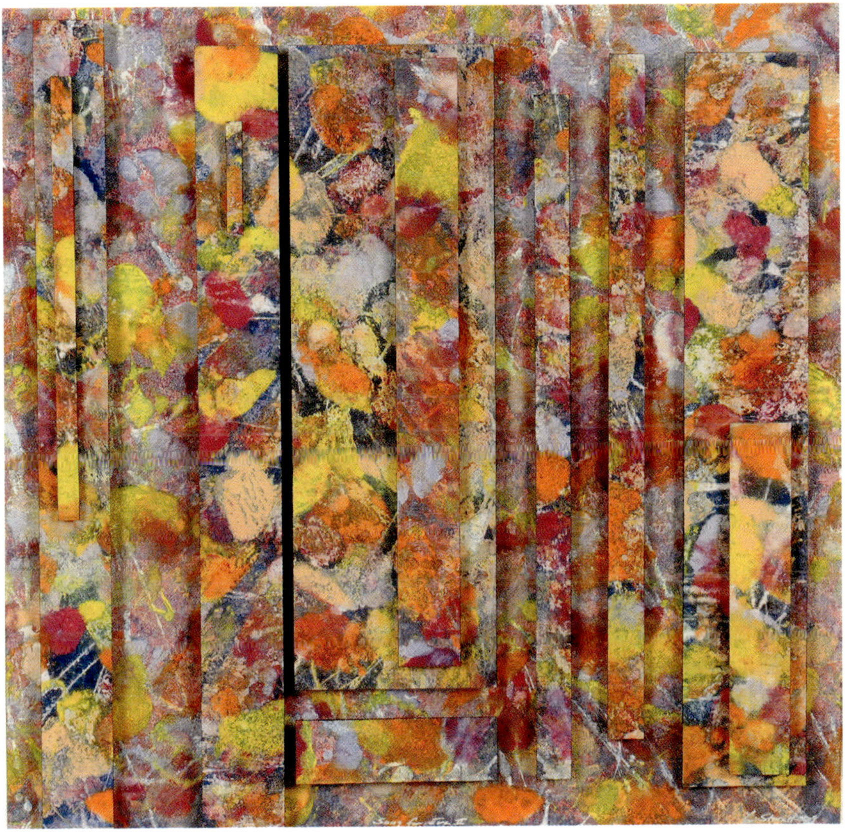

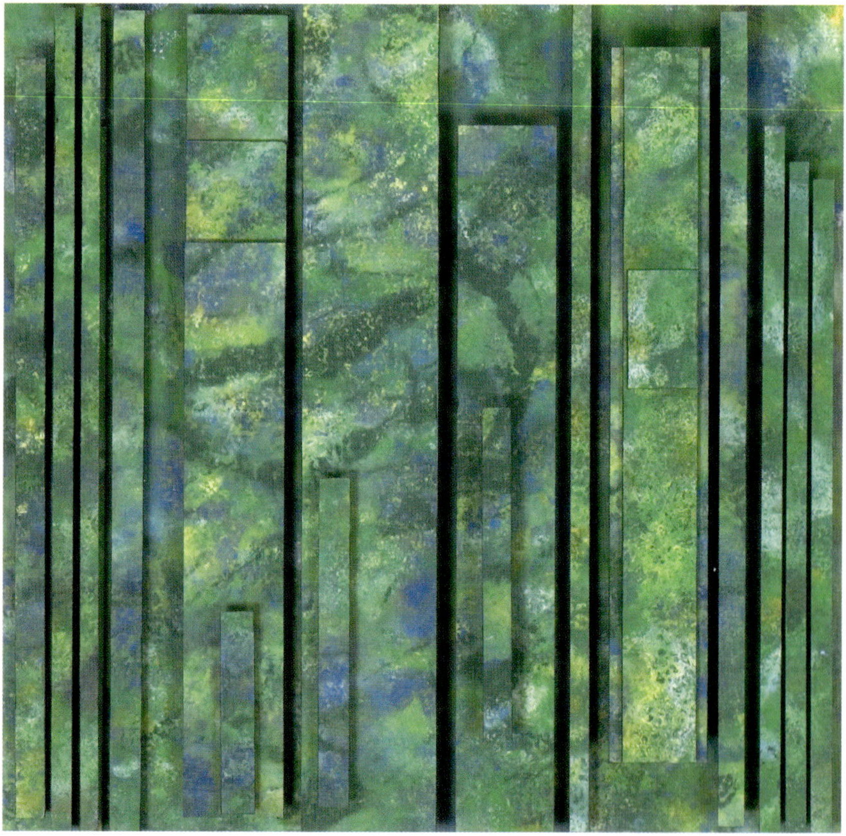

Blue Grass Meadow, 2012

Silkscreen monoprint collage
25 1/4 x 25 1/4 in.

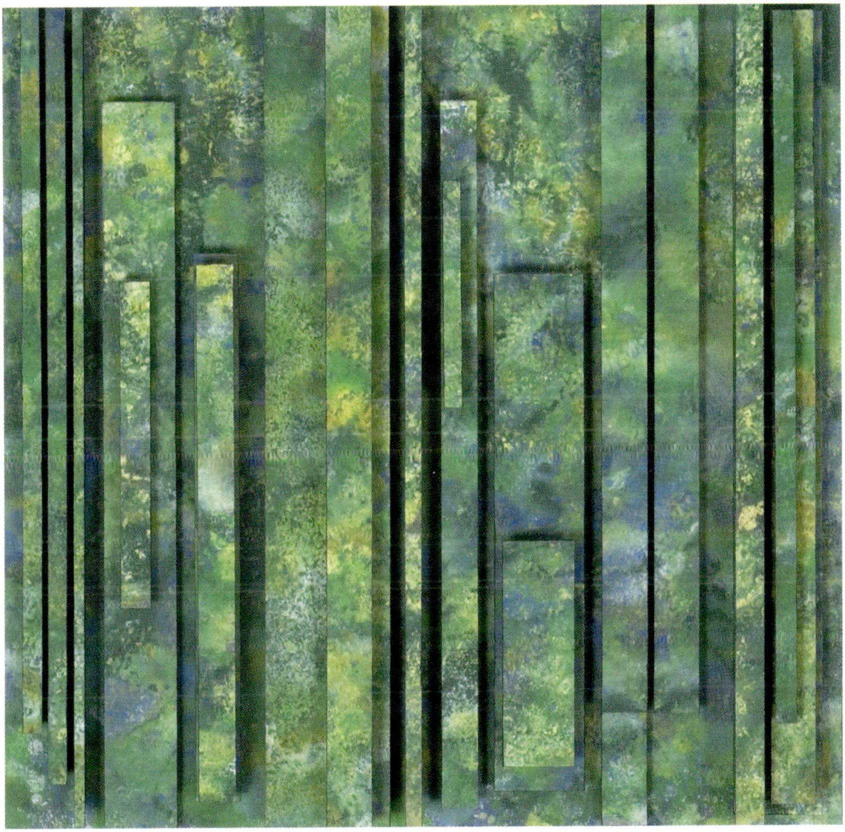

A... Whispering, 2012
Silkscreen monoprint collage
25 1/4 x 25 1/4 in.

Metaphor I, 2005
Graphite pencil drawing
19 1/4 x 18 3/4 in.

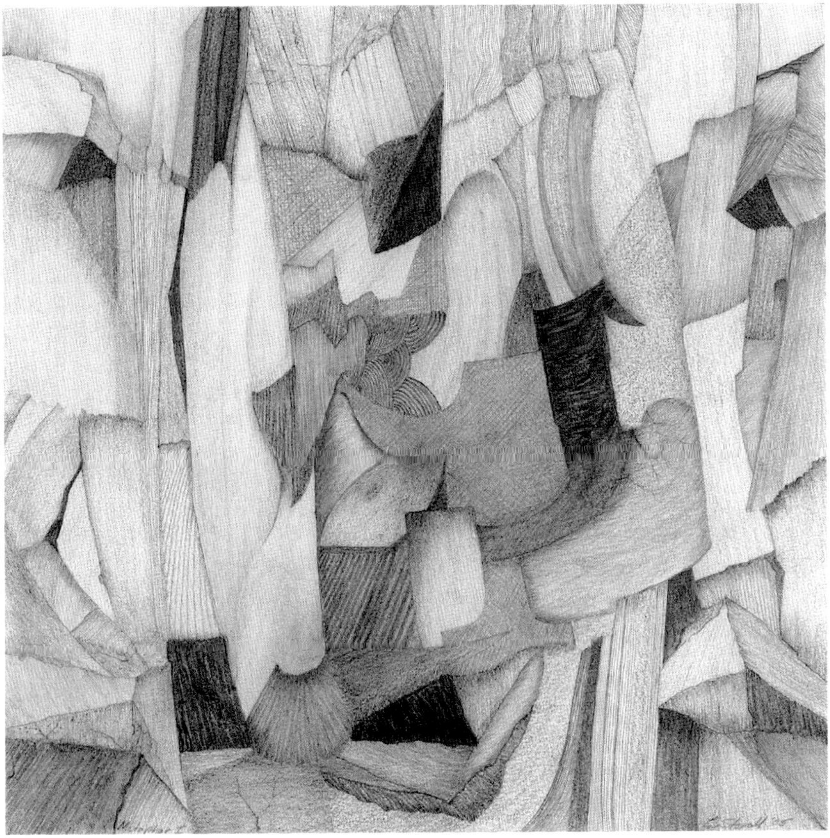

Lined Cattleyas and Bauhinias, 2006

70 Graphite pencil drawing

32 1/2 x 44 in.

Next: *Lined Cattleyas and Bauhinias*, detail

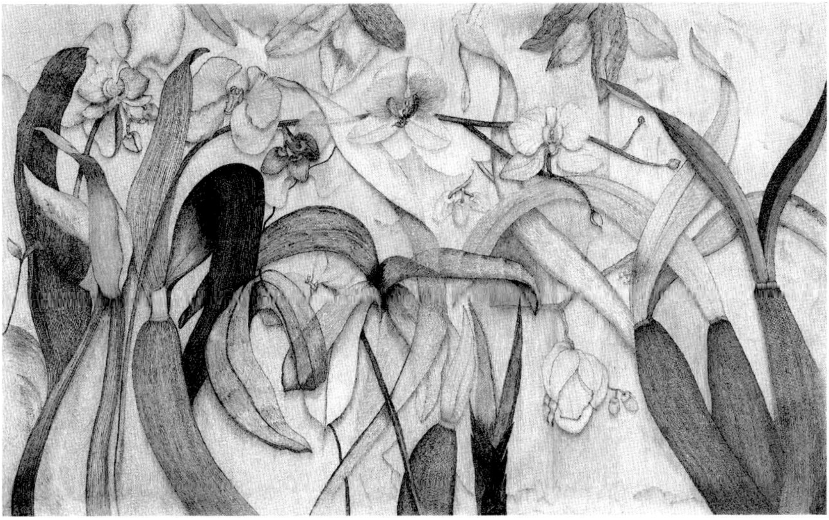

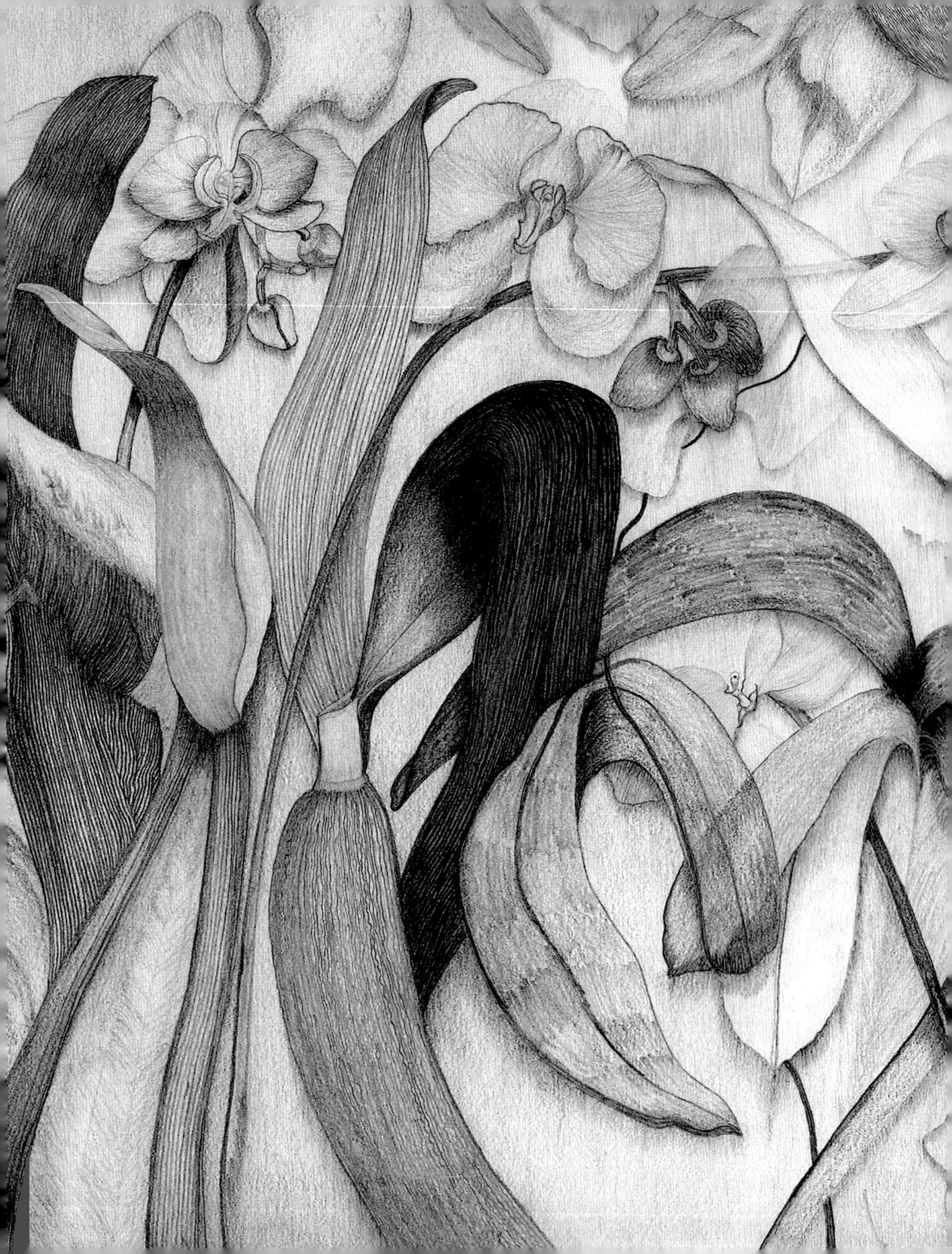

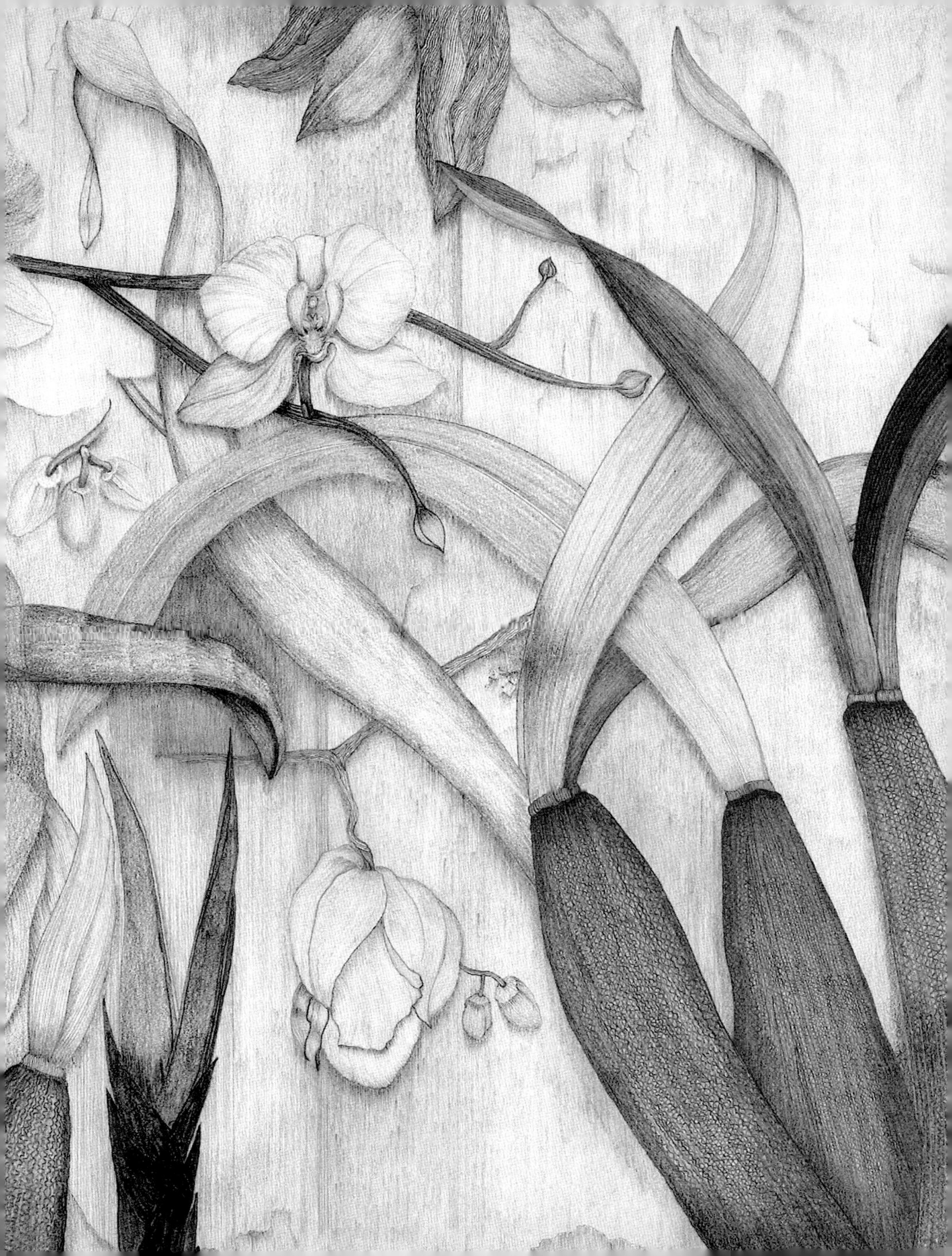

The Persistence of Nature, 2006
Graphite pencil drawing
32 1/2 x 44 in.

Next: *The Persistence of Nature*, detail

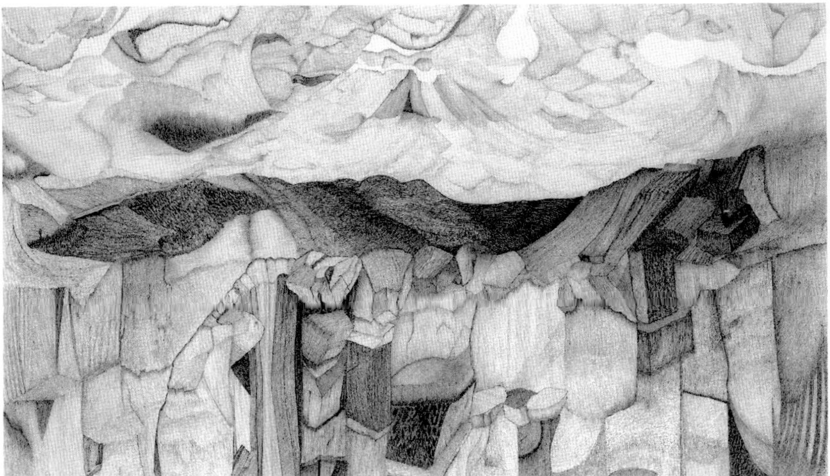

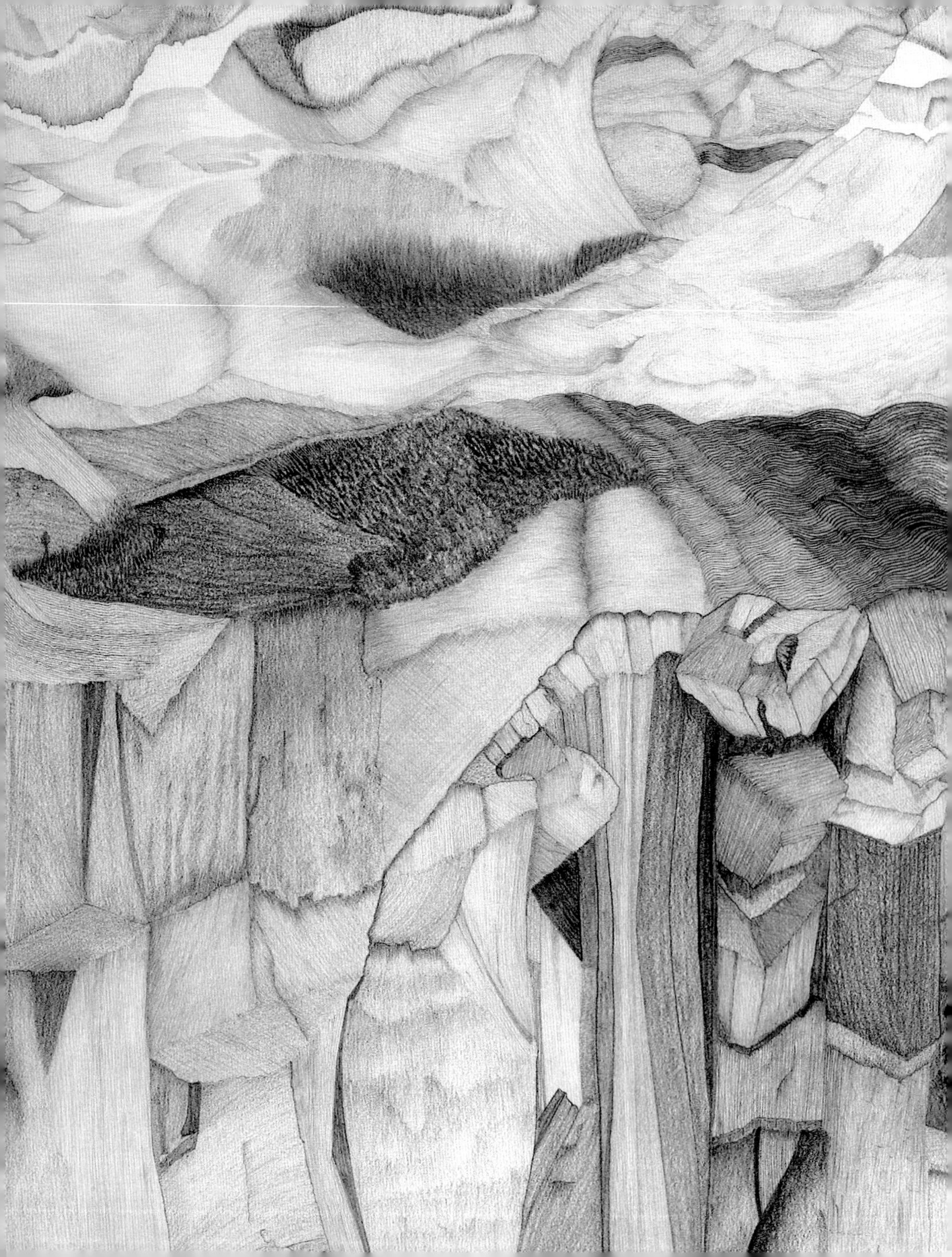

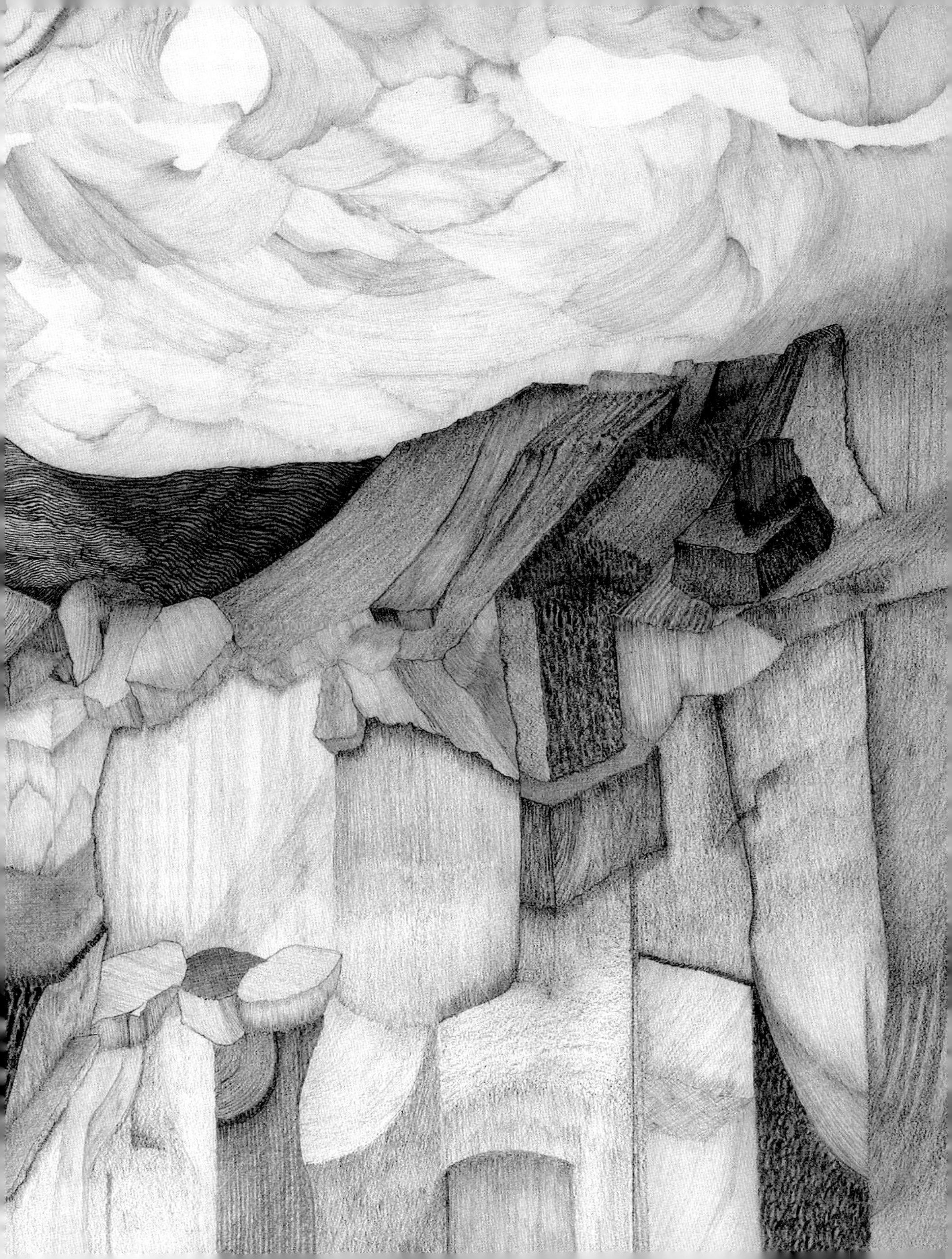

78

Sally's Field, Planted, 2012
Silkscreen monoprint
32 x 51 1/2 in.

Next: *Sally's Field, Planted*, detail

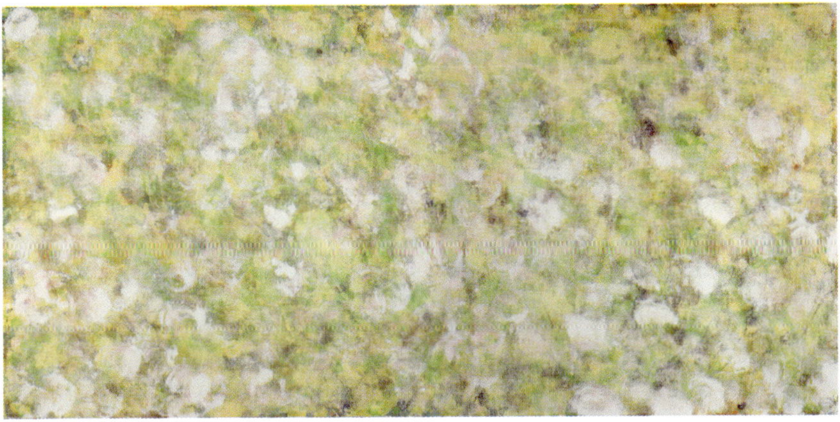

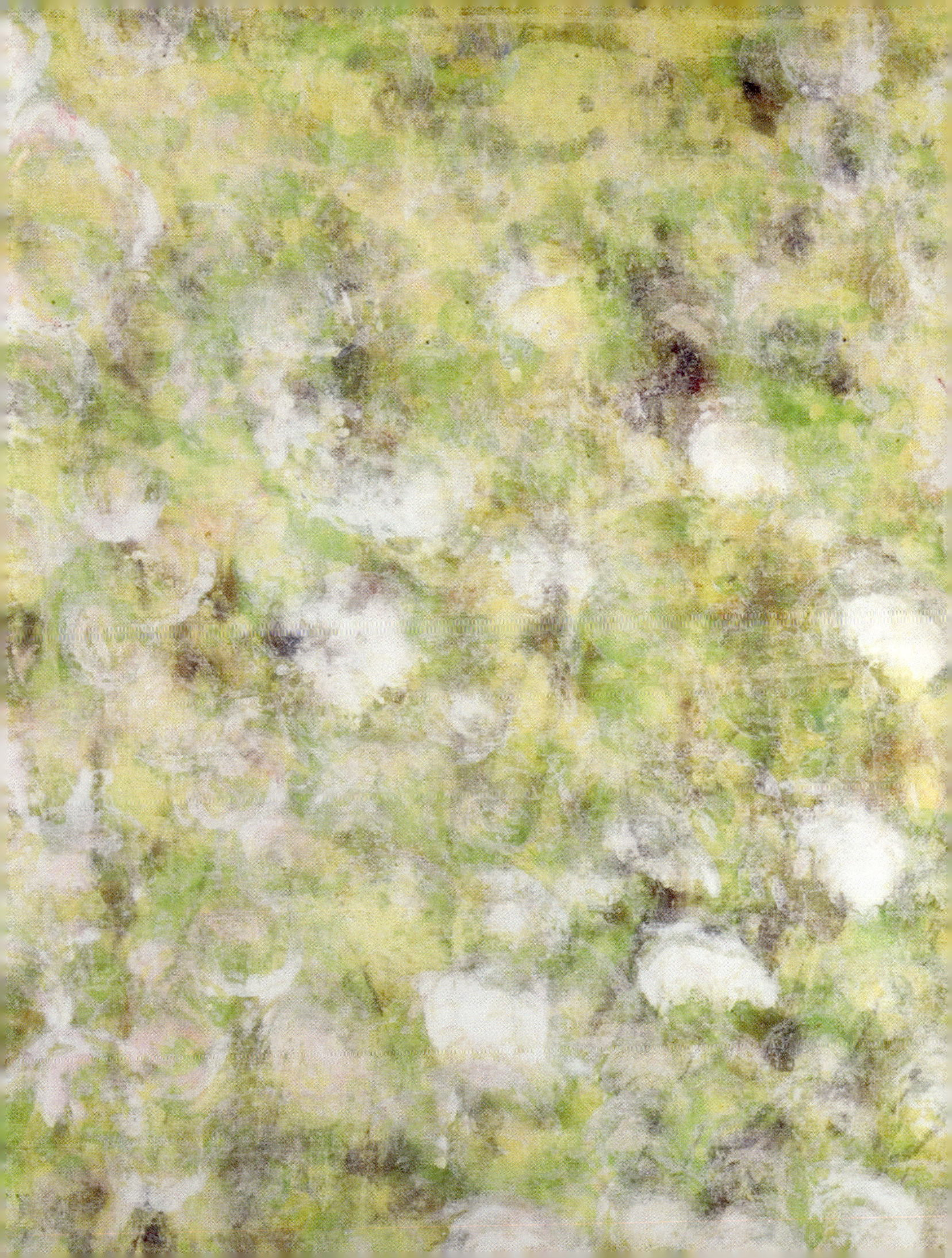

Sweet Tea, 2012
Silkscreen monoprint
32 x 51 1/2 in.

Next: *Sweet Tea*, detail

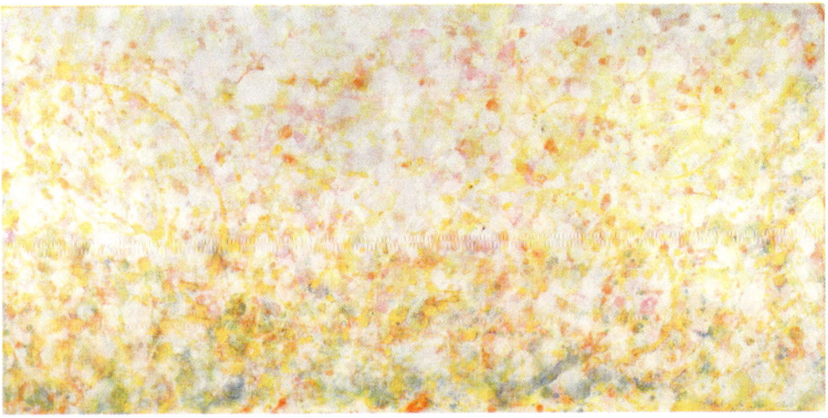

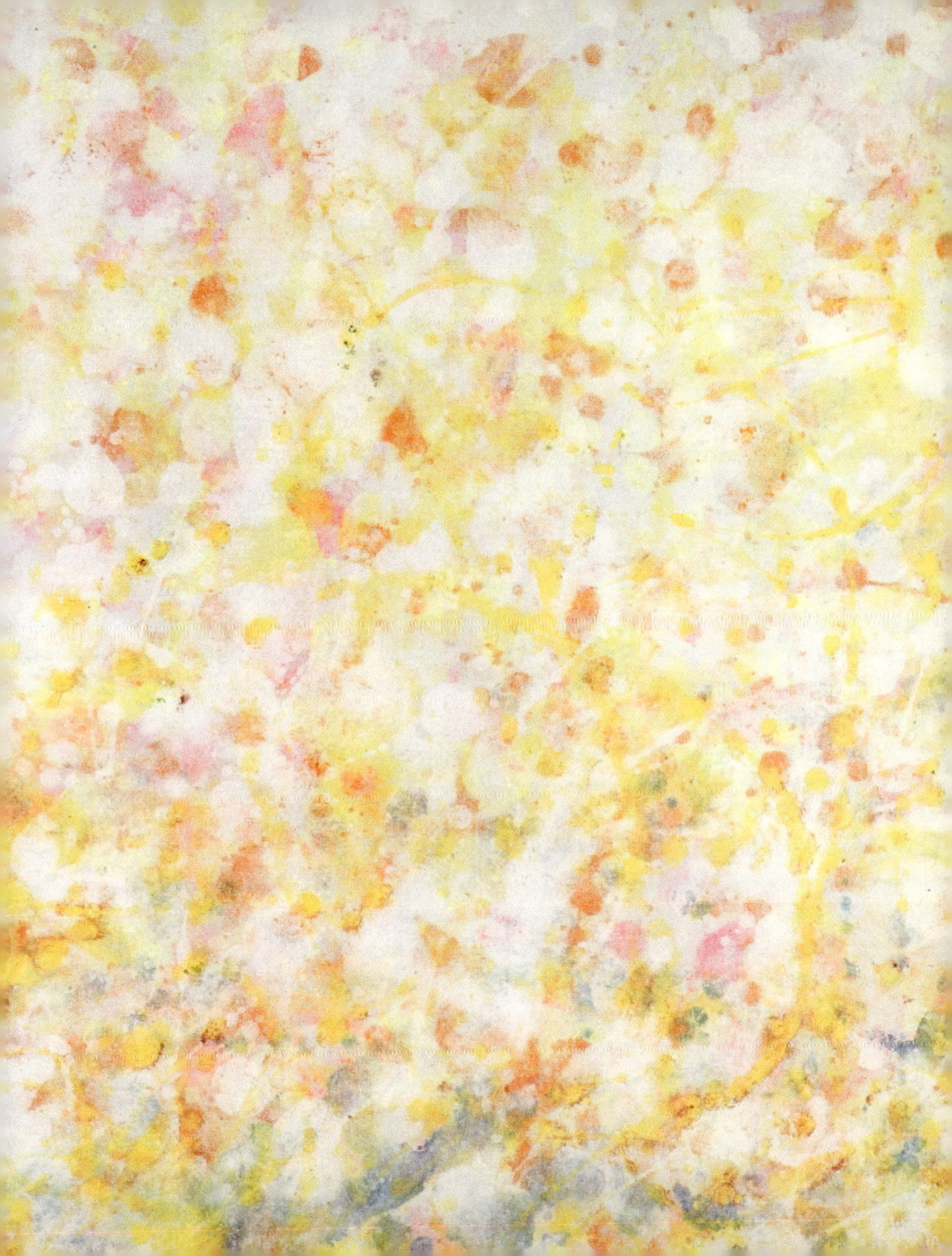

Apricot Afternoon, 2012

Silkscreen Monoprint
32 x 51 1/2 in.

Next: *Apricot Afternoon*, detail

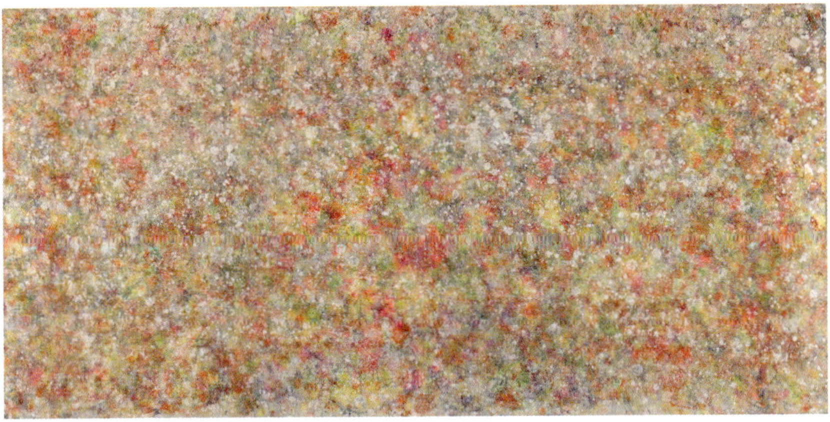

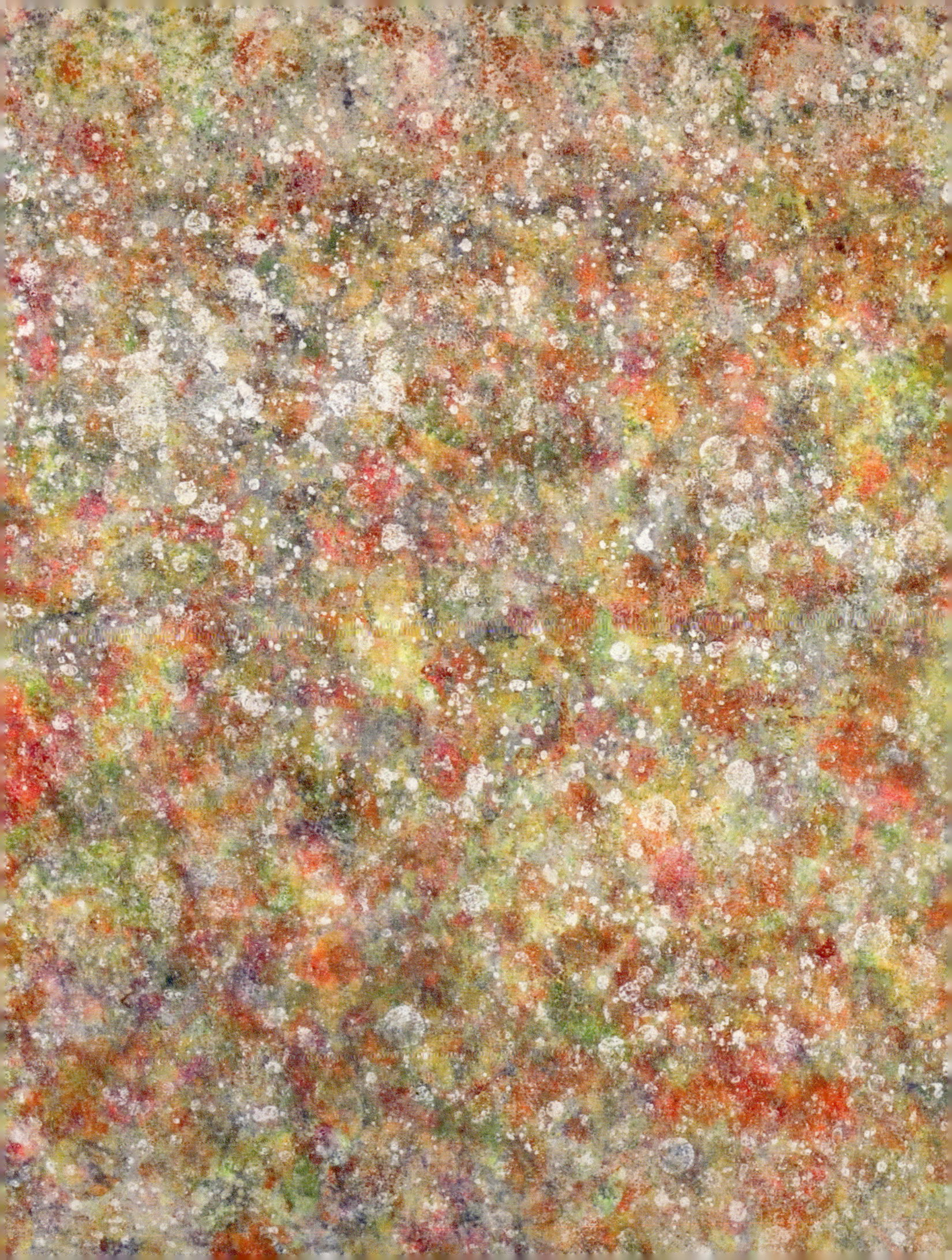

Black Magic, 2010

Silkscreen monoprint

32 x 51 1/2 in.

Next: *Black Magic*, detail

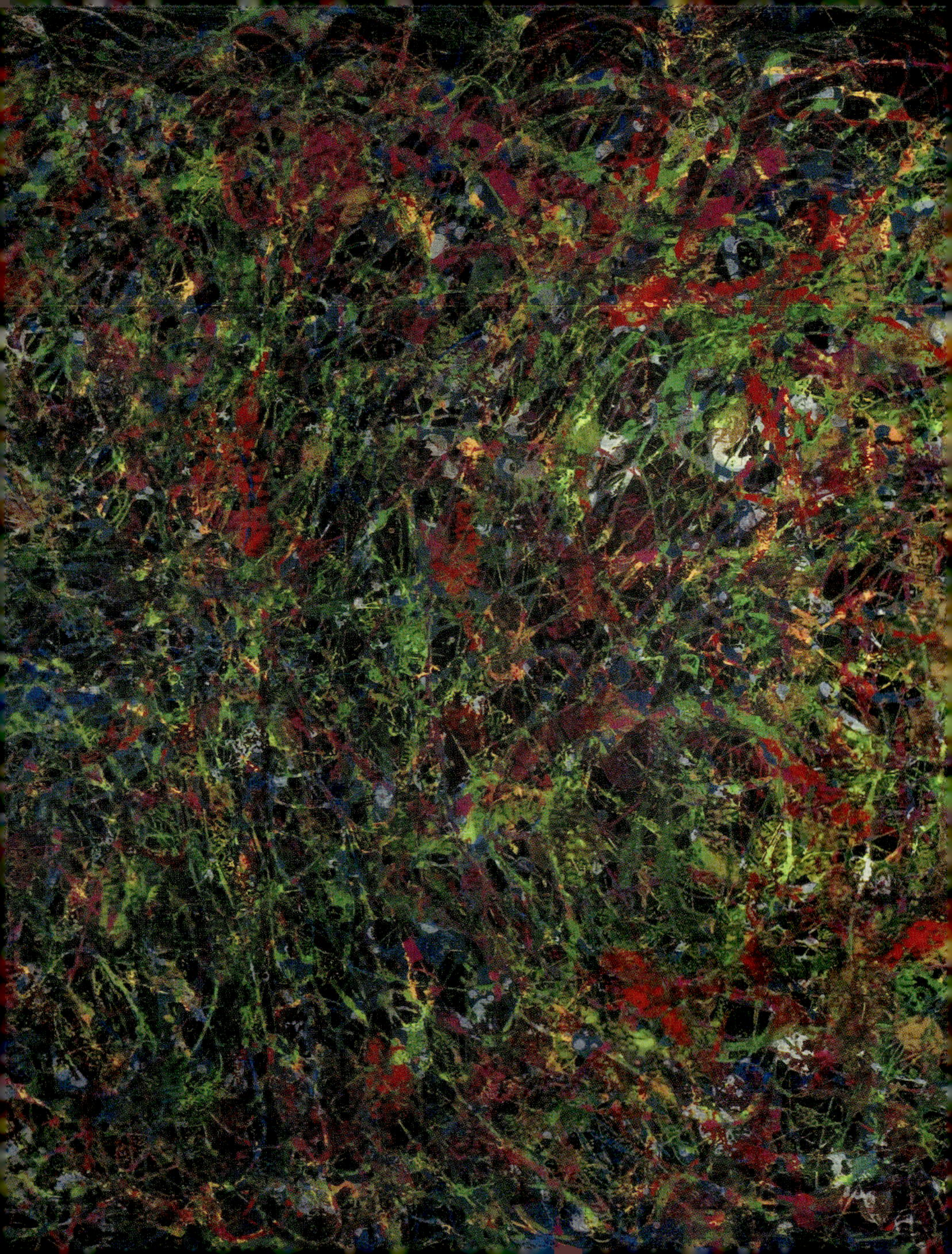

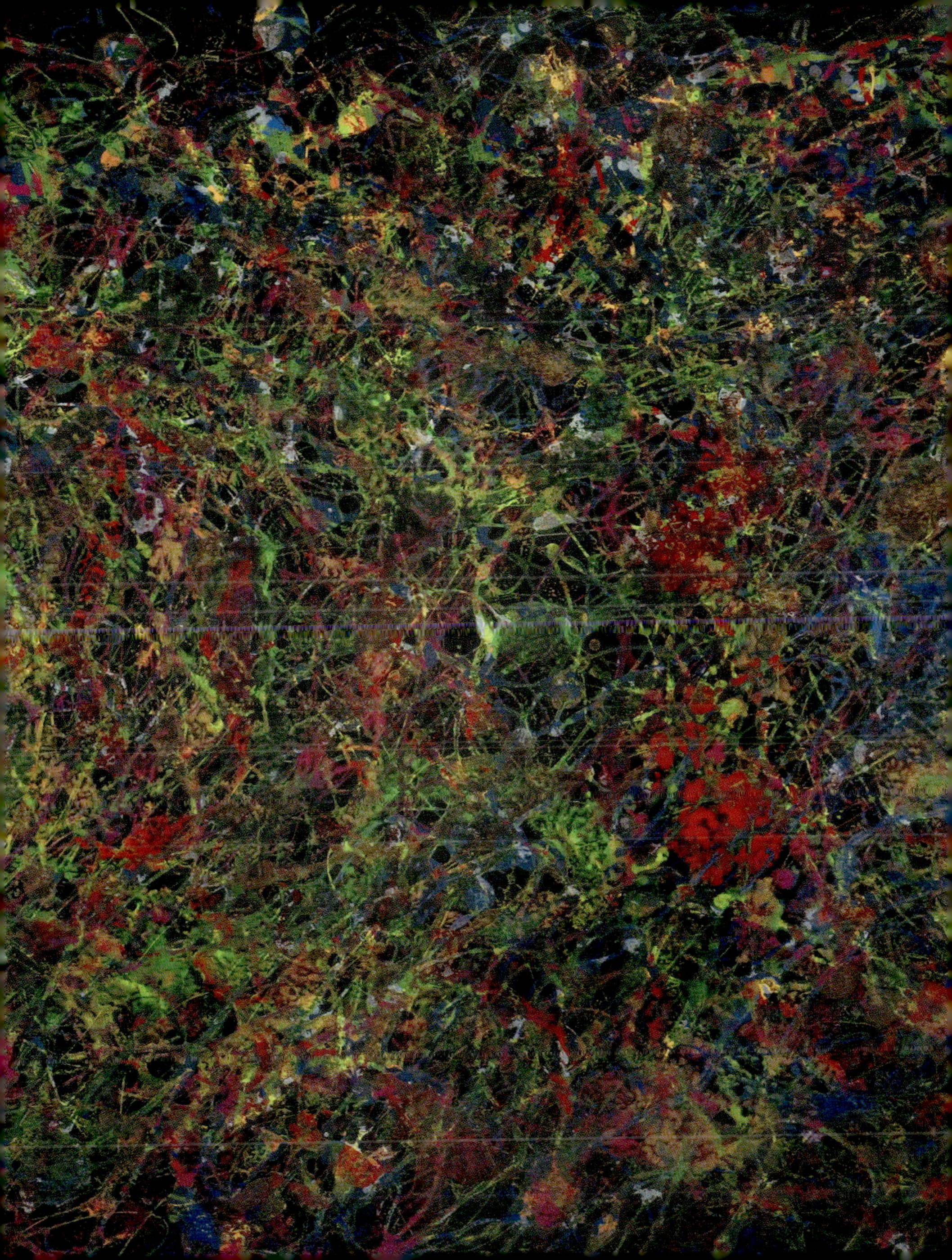

Sun Field, 2010

Silkscreen monoprint

41 x 53 in.

Next: *Sun Field*, detail

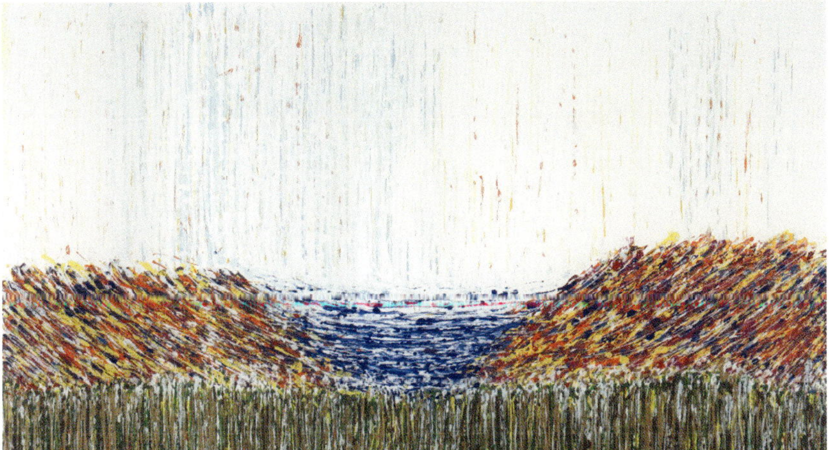

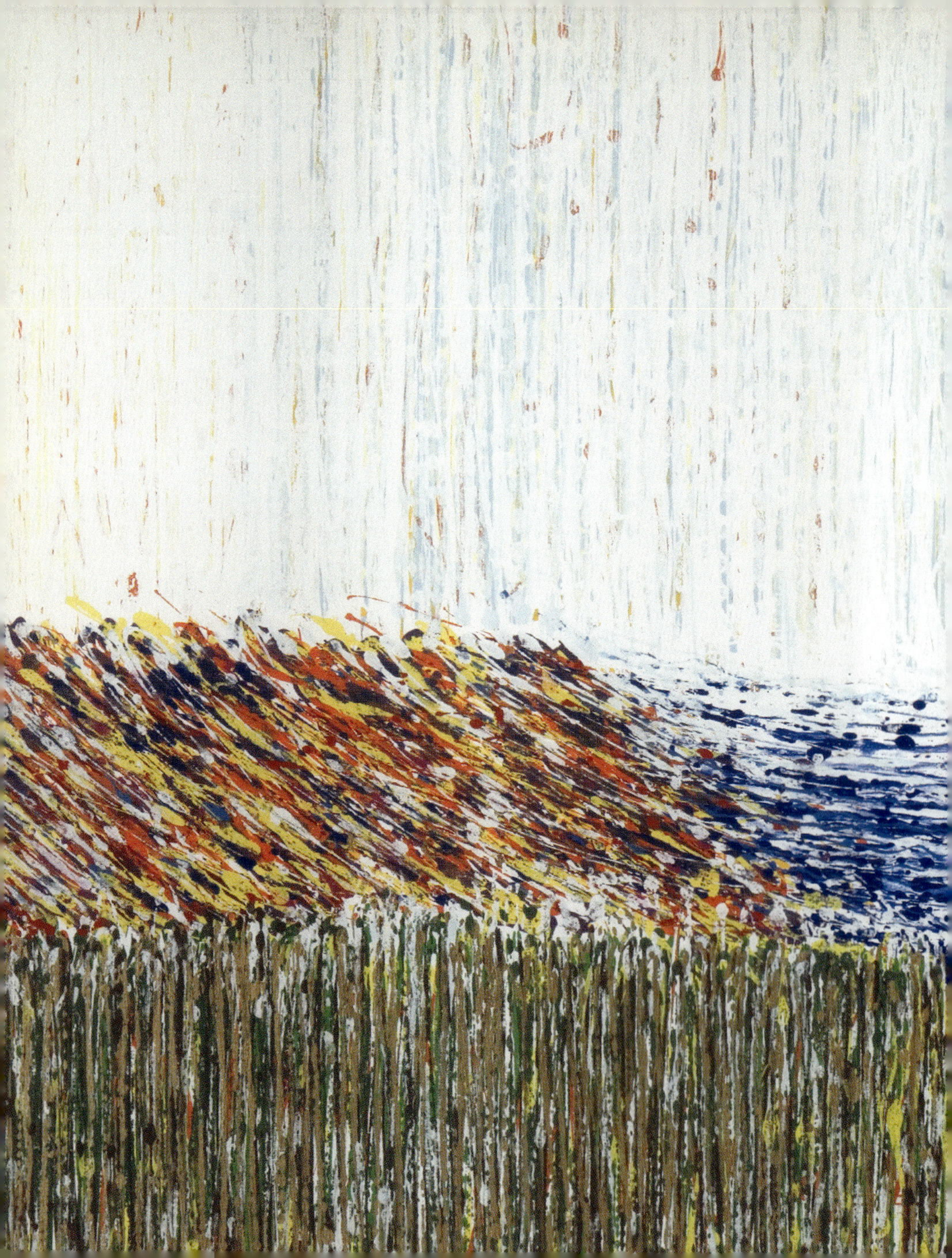

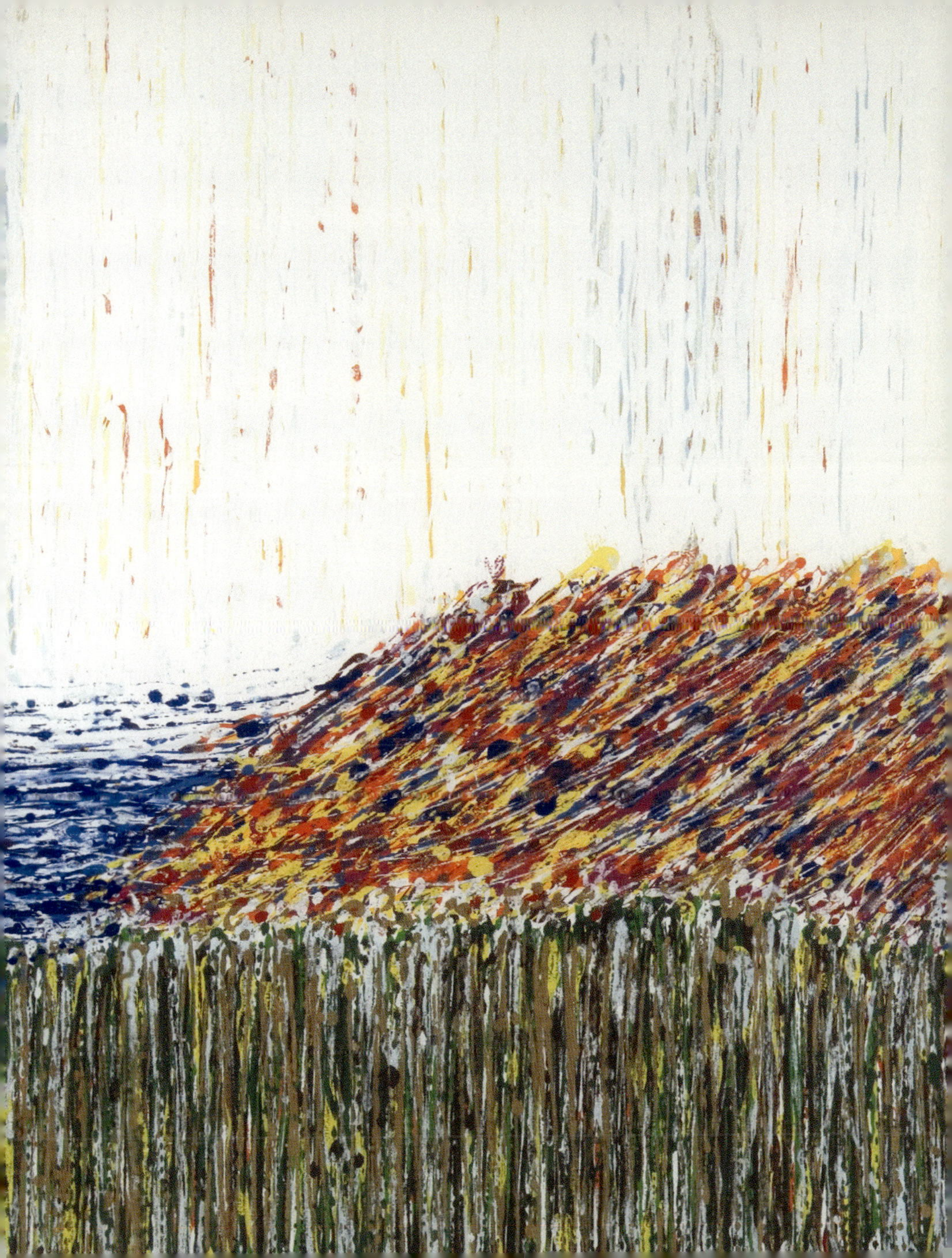

Night Fall, 2010
Silkscreen monoprint
32 x 51 1/2 in.

Next: *Night Fall*, detail

Vespers, 2010
102 Silkscreen monoprint
29 3/4 x 49 1/4 in.

Next: *Vespers*, detail

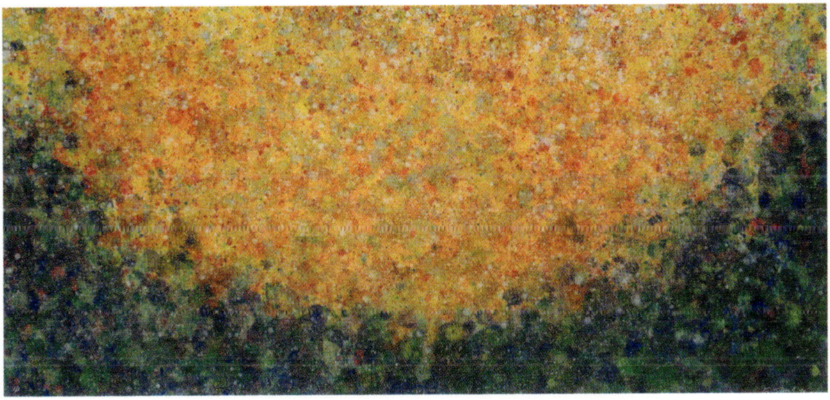

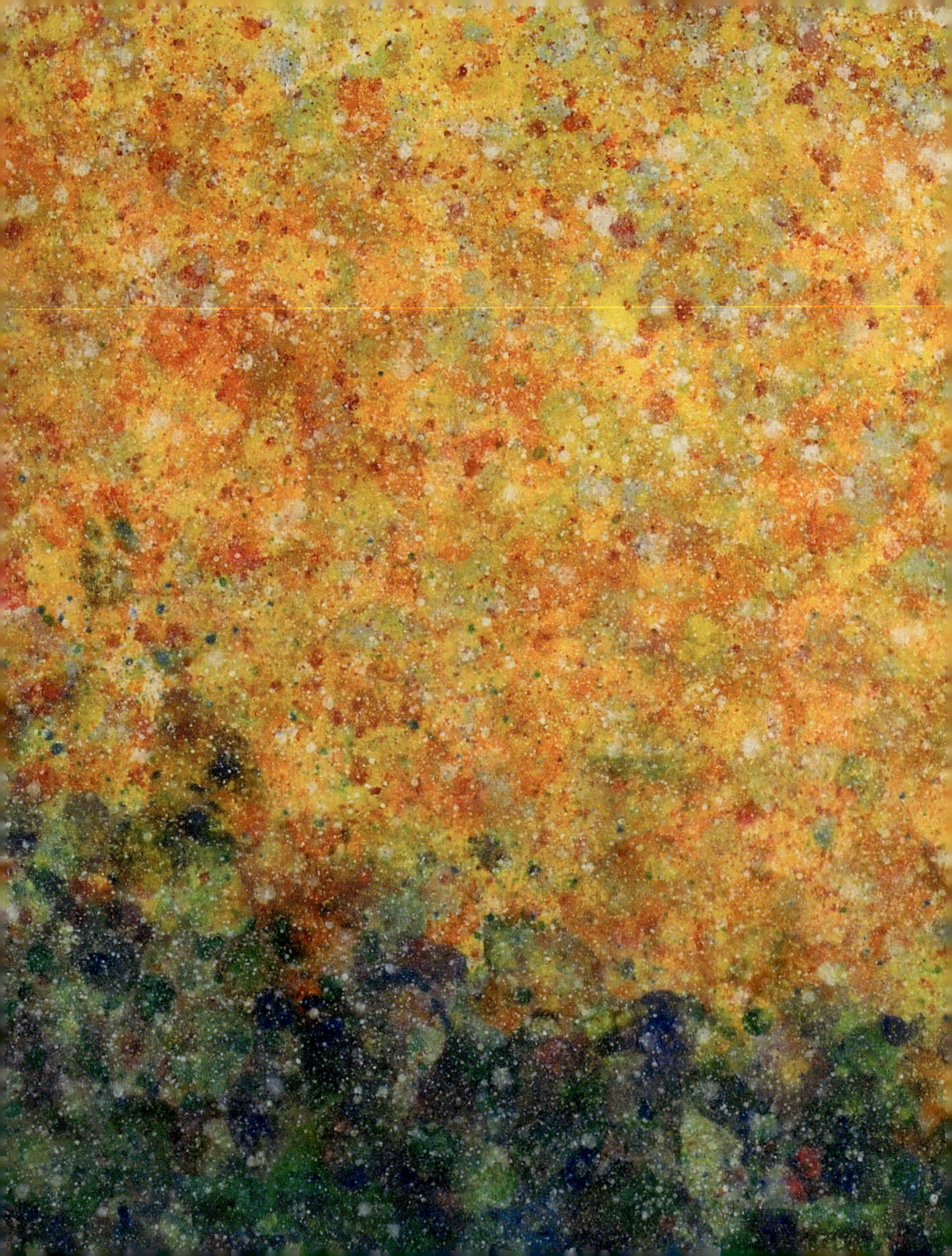

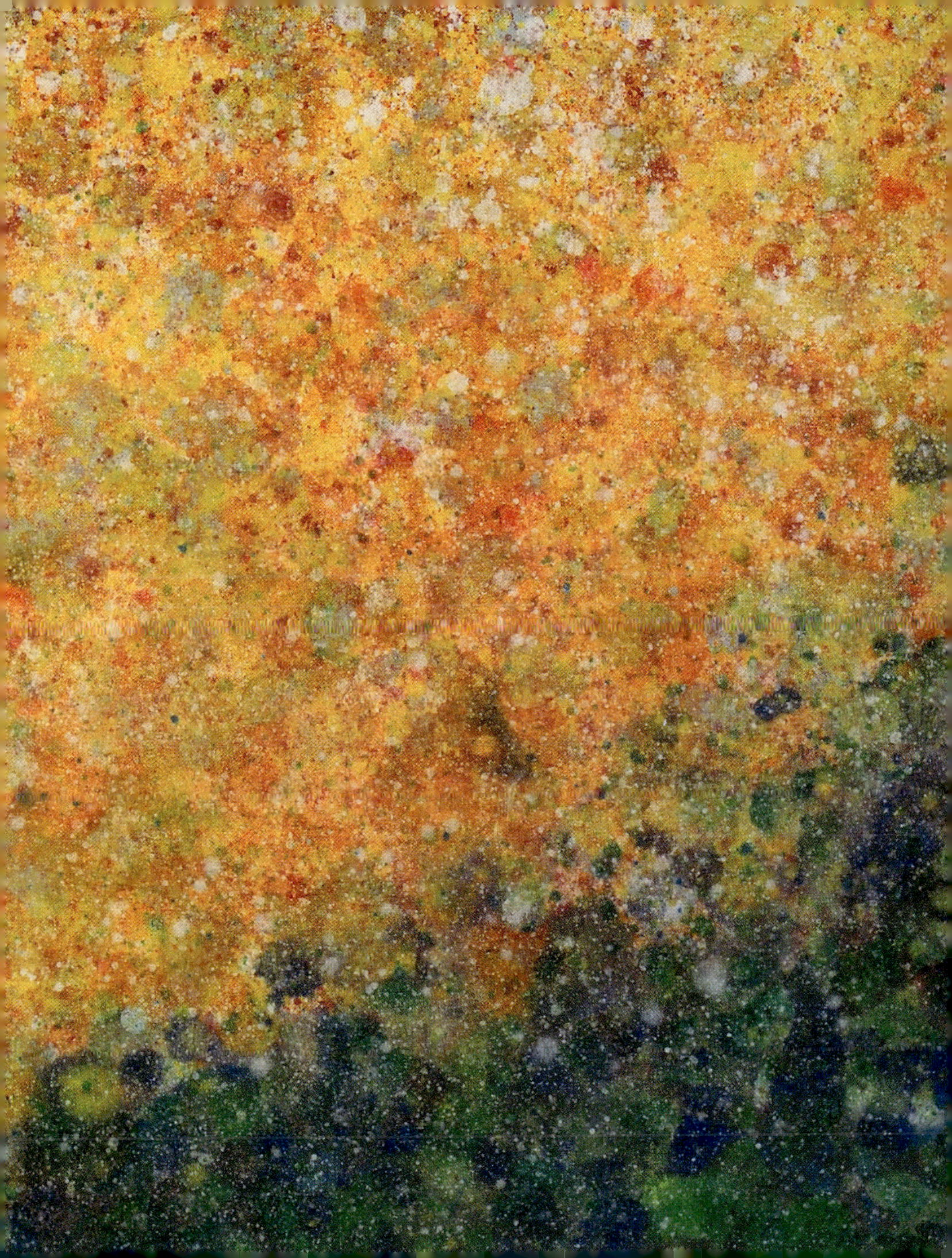

Pomegranate, 2012

Silkscreen monoprint

32 x 51 1/2 in.

Next: *Pomegranate*, detail

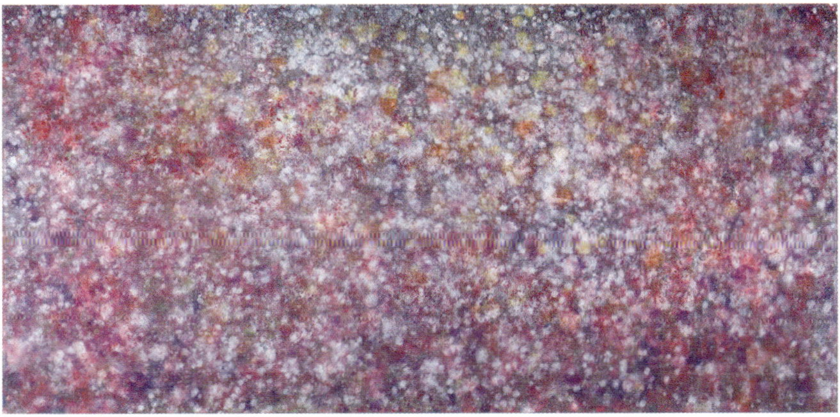

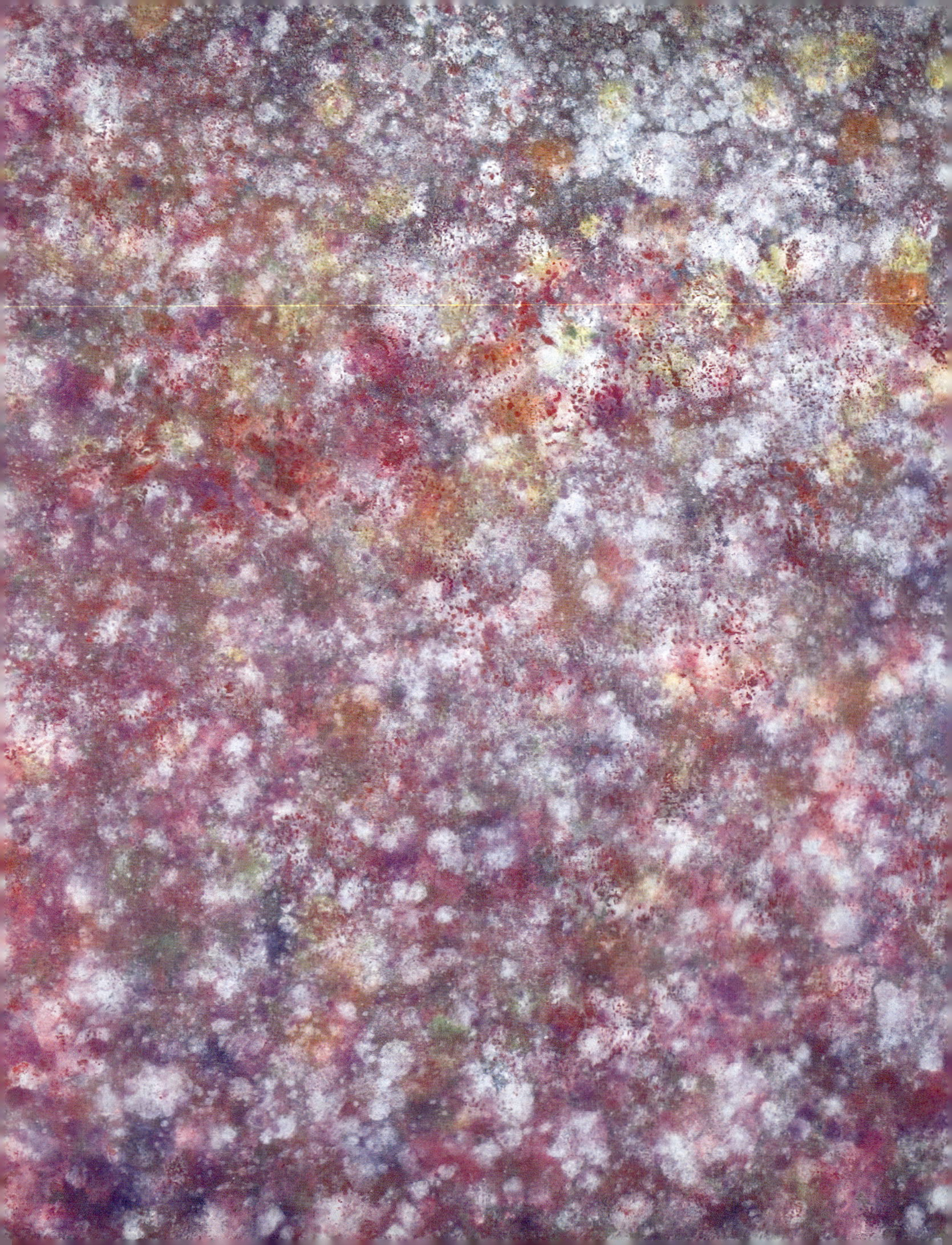

Terce, 2012

Silkscreen monoprint

32 x 51 1/2 in.

Next: *Terce*, detail

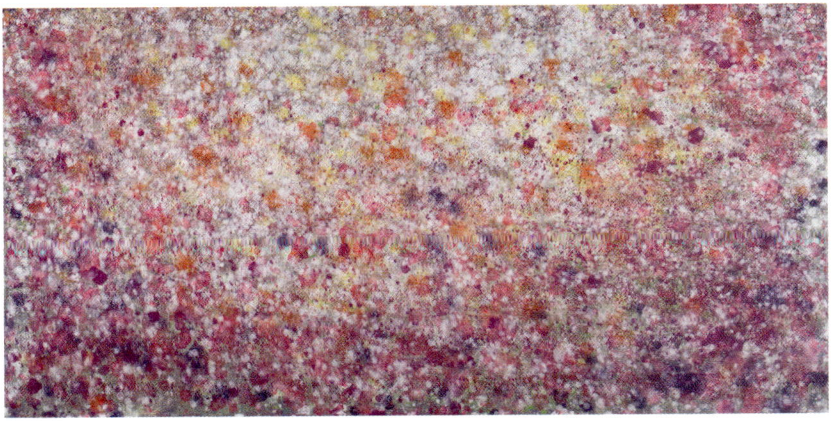

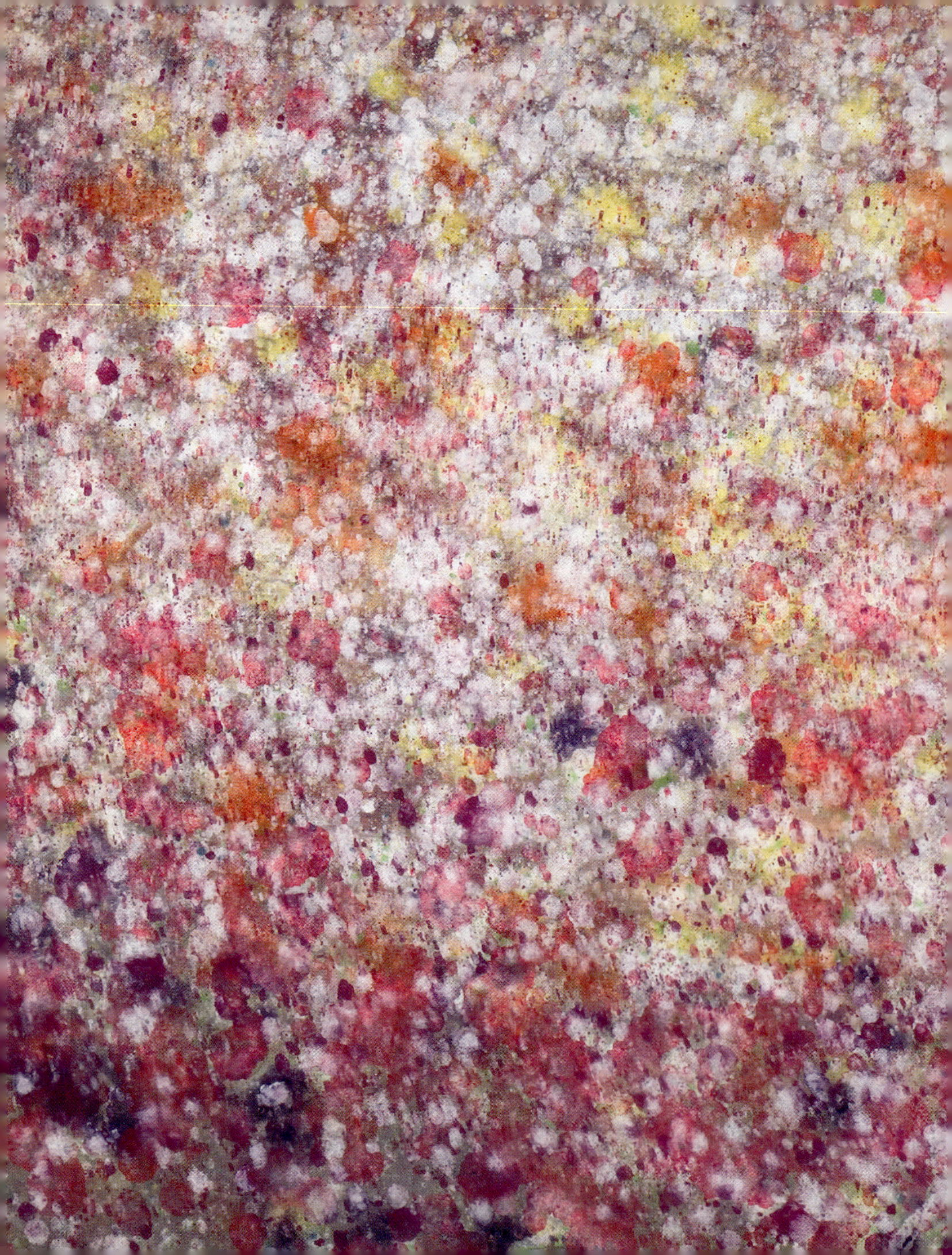

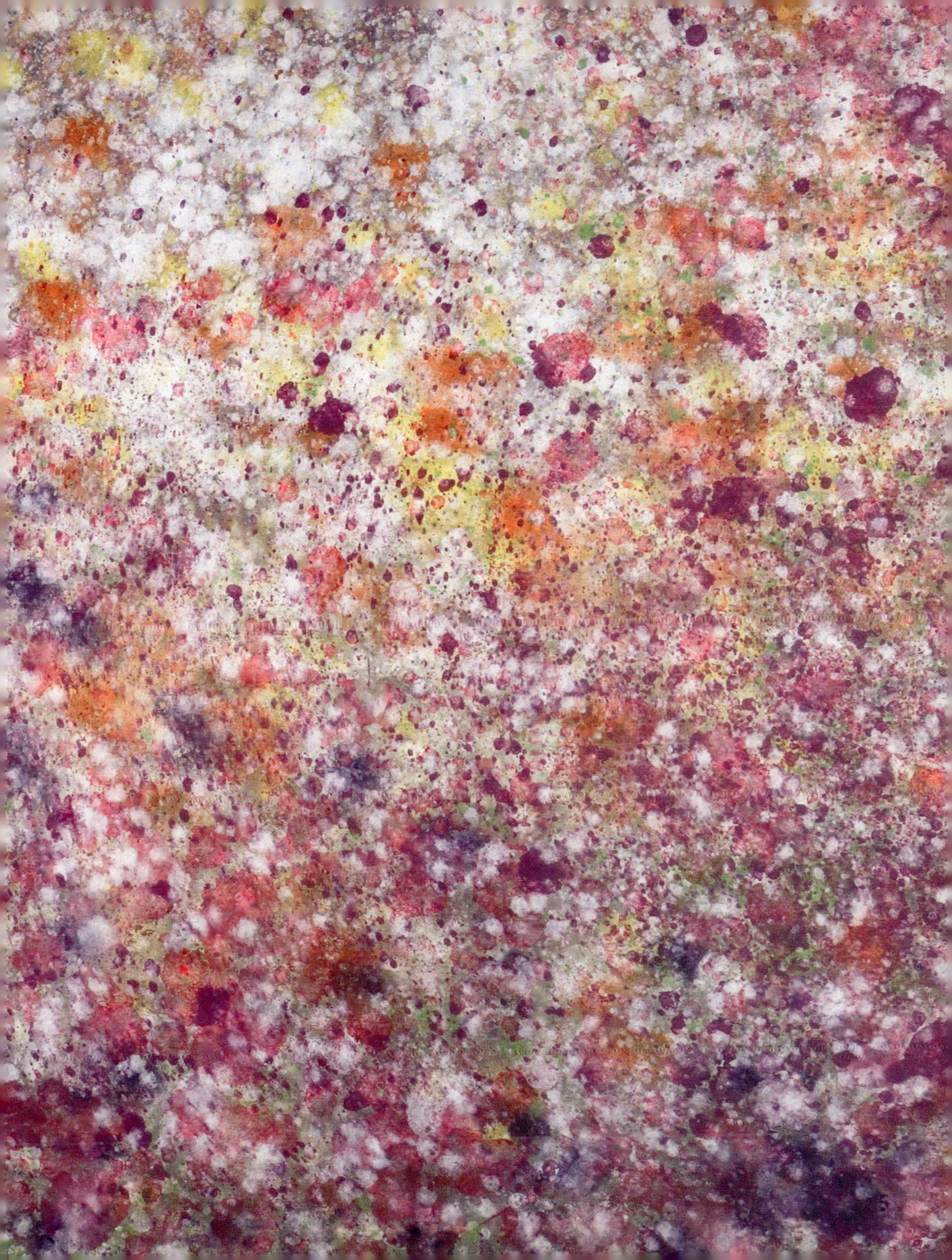

Scarlet Calligraphy, 2009

Silkscreen monoprint
32 x 51 in.
Collection of Di Bagley Stovall

Next: *Scarlet Calligraphy*, detail

Brindle, 2011

Silkscreen monoprint

32 x 51 1/2 in.

Next: *Brindle*, detail

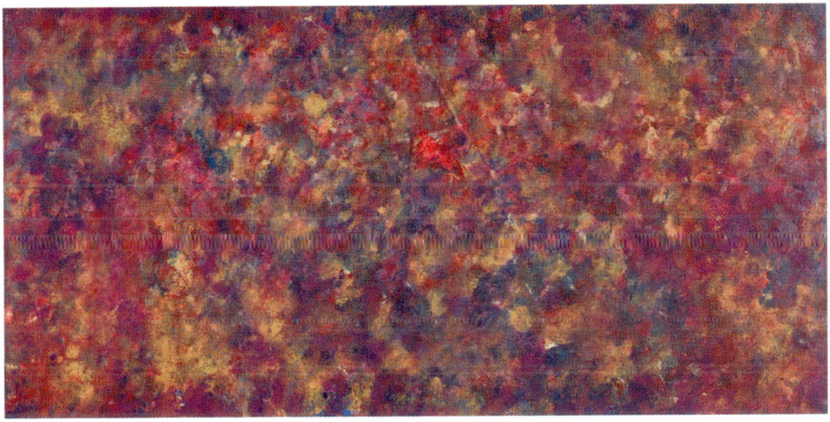

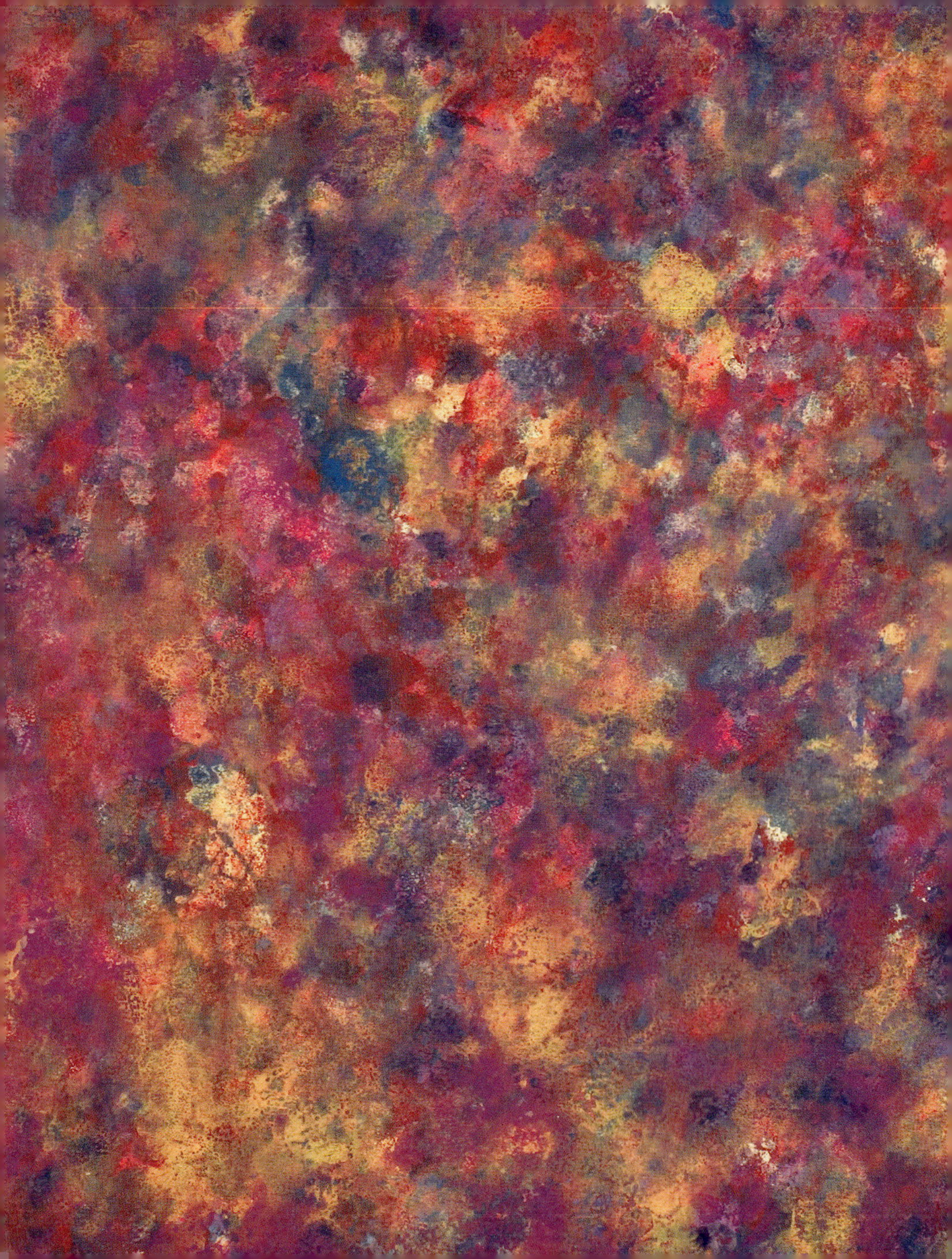

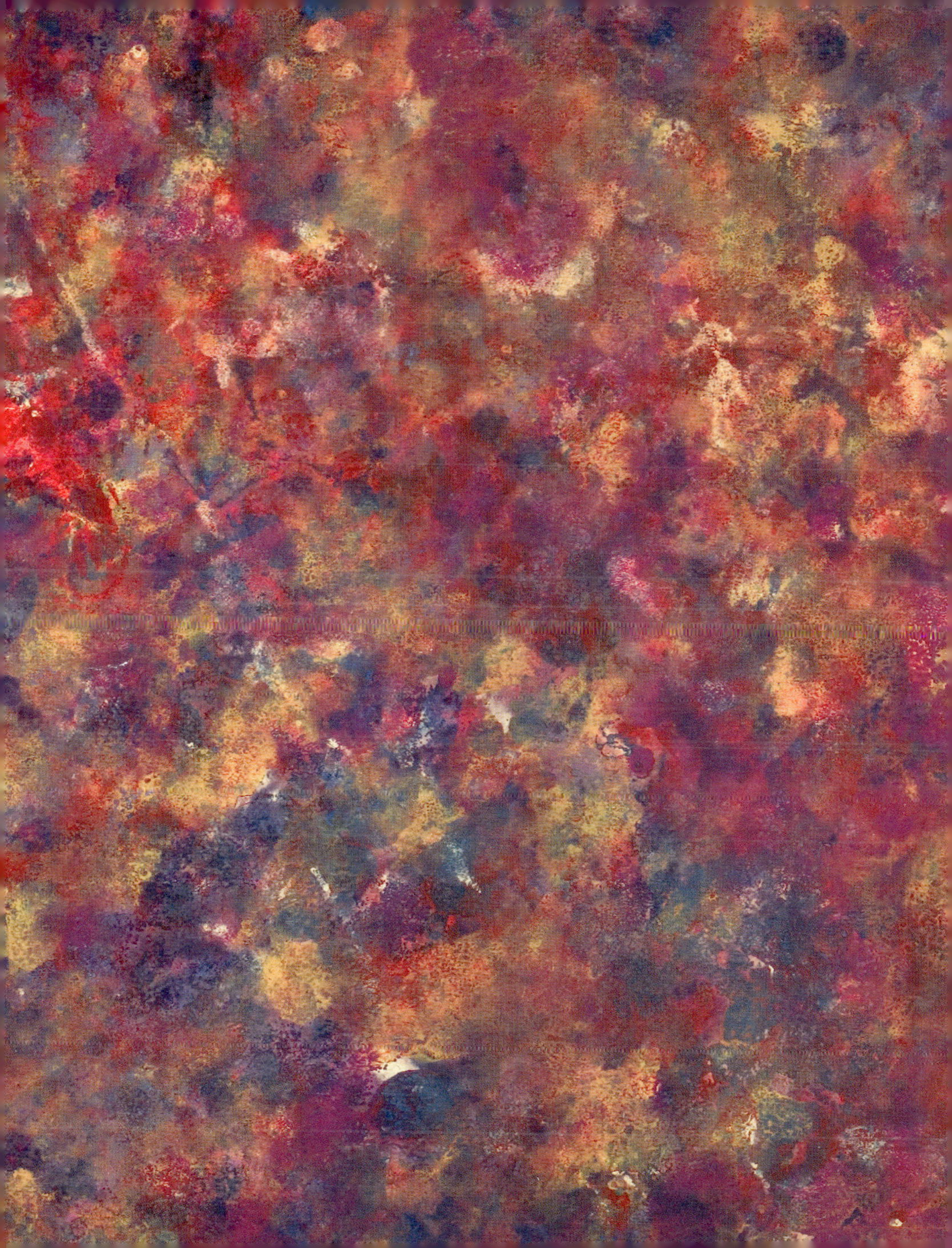

THANKS

Neil Kerwin, president, American University
Peter Starr, dean, College of Arts and Sciences, American University
Jack Rasmussen, director and curator, American University Museum
The Katzen Arts Center, American University

Christopher Addison
Jody Bergstresser
Sally and Tersh Boasberg
Ed Dickey
Lisa Farrell
Craig Fuller
Idris Hallack
Katherine MacDiarmid
Rachael Mahr
Samantha Marques-Mordorfsky
Cornelia Marsh
Jim Miller
Ann Miller-Lee
Audrey Morgan
Kate Pincus
Will Reid
Faith Reid
Grace Reid
Aaron Sinift
Anne Smith
Greg Staley
Ed Starleper
Leni Stern
Danny Stern
Jennifer Stewart
Di Bagley Stovall
Will Stovall
Calea Stovall-Reid
Holly Tank
William Upton
Sheila and Willy Walker
Bruce Wick
Zacherey Willis
John Woo